Lincoln Bible Institute

P9-CEG-561

OUTLINES OF JUDAISM

A MANUAL OF THE BELIEFS, CEREMONIES, ETHICS AND PRACTICES
OF
THE JEWISH PEOPLE

By

SAMUEL PRICE

Rabbi, Congregation Beth El
Springfield, Mass.

BLOCH PUBLISHING COMPANY

NEW YORK : 1946

Copyright, 1946, by

BLOCH PUBLISHING CO., INC.

PRINTED IN THE UNITED STATES OF AMERICA

296
P94

3845

To

FANNY PRICE

MY FAITHFUL HELPMATE

PREFACE

For thirty-three years I instructed the Confirmation Classes of the Congregation Beth El, in Springfield, Mass., in the tenets and practices of Judaism. For thirty years I tried to discover an adequate textbook for the teachings of Judaism but failed to find one. I found it necessary to follow the example of many of my colleagues in the rabbinate and make up a set of "Outlines" for use in the classroom. The material contained in this book is based on those "Outlines."

During my long ministry I have come in contact with many types of Jews. One member of my Congregation, a mystic and a scholar, told me that he was opposed to religious ceremonies and that he was a staunch believer in Jewish fundamentals, but when asked as to what the fundamental creeds of Judaism were, he had no answer. Another member of my Congregation, an observant Jew, was anxious to instruct his son in Jewish ceremonials, but could not do it effectively because his own knowledge of these ceremonials was superficial and fragmentary. A third member of my Congregation, a great admirer of the prophets and of ethical Judaism, was astonished when I brought to his attention the fact that in his vast library there was not a single book on the Ethics of Judaism written in readable, simple language.

A Gentile woman recently came to me and expressed a sincere desire to embrace Judaism. I consented to her request and told her that she would have to study the teachings and practices of Judaism. However, when she asked for a textbook to study from, I had to admit to her that a single book containing a complete presentation of the principles, ceremonies, and ethics of Judaism was not available in America.

This book is therefore intended to serve as a textbook and guide for the religious school, for the home, and for prospective newcomers to the Jewish fold. It is presented, as far as possible, in the "Outlines" form. Each chapter is divided into a series of main topics, or headlines, and each topic is followed by explanations and comments. All available material, culled from the Bible, the Talmud, the Midrash, the Shulchan Aruch, etc., was utilized in the preparation of these "Outlines." The attached "Bibliography" gives the sources of information, and the "Glossary" contains a short biography of each person whose name appears in this volume. When Hebrew words are transliterated into English, the popular Ashkenazic form is generally used. The spelling is nearest to the way the words are pronounced.

The material presented in this volume deals primarily with Judaism as a religion. Though I agree, to a large extent, with Dr. Mordecai M. Kaplan's theory that Judaism is a complete civilization, yet I maintain that religion, as a whole, dominates the scene in Jewish life. To quote Dr. Kaplan, "If the glory of a civilization consists in the uniqueness of its contribution to human culture, then religion was, and will remain, the glory of the Jewish civilization. Take religion out and Judaism becomes an empty shell."

Many a Jew, upon reading this material, may exclaim, "I don't believe in this, or in that," but that type of argument is to be expected. It is difficult to present the beliefs and observances of Judaism with dogmatic words of finality, for ours is a living, changing religion. It was subjected to many changes throughout the ages and it has been especially revised and classified in the last one hundred years. Nevertheless, Judaism has basic principles to which the observant Jew has subscribed from the days of the Talmud to the present, and these principles of traditional Judaism are usually adhered to in the presentation which follows.

I acknowledge with gratitude the advice and assistance given to me by the following colleagues and friends: Rabbi Herschel Levin, of Sinai Temple, Springfield; Rabbi Isaac Klein of Congregation Kodimoh, Springfield; Rev. Ivan G. Grimshaw, of the American International College, Springfield; Dr. Herman Hailperin, Rabbi, Congregation Tree of Life, Pittsburgh, Pa.; Rabbi Morris Silverman, of the Emanuel Synagogue, Hartford, Conn.; Dr. Israel M. Goldman, Rabbi, Temple Emanuel, Providence, R.I.; Rabbi Arnold A. Lasker, my son-in-law, now Chaplain in the U.S. Army. I am also thankful to my daughters, Lillian P. Brill and Miriam P. Lasker, for their encouragement and valuable suggestions.

It is my hope and prayer that this book may serve as a guide and lead many people not only to the knowledge of Judaism, but also to the observance of its laws and traditions.

SAMUEL PRICE.

Springfield, Mass.
Nissan, 5706.
April, 1946.

INTRODUCTION

JUDAISM IS THE RELIGION OF THE JEWISH PEOPLE.

Our people are called (a) Hebrews, the descendants of Abraham, the first Hebrew; (b) Israelites, the children of Jacob who was given the honorary name of Israel (champion of God); (c) Jews, or Judeans, descendants of Judah, the only one of the original twelve tribes which survived the days of the Babylonian exile. Judaism, the religion of the children of Judah, comprises a series of laws and ceremonies which regulate the religious life of the Jewish people.

RELIGION TEACHES US OUR DUTIES TO GOD AND TO OUR FELLOW MEN.

To some people religion is a matter of denominational loyalty and of occasional worship, but to the Jewish people it is a complete way of life. Unlike philosophy, religion does not seek to prove things; it aims to inspire faith, not to demonstrate facts. Its purpose is to raise man to a higher plane of living and to lead him toward godliness and perfection. "Ye shall be holy, for I, the Lord your God, am holy" (Lev. 19:2).

To describe the many phases of Judaism—its teachings and practices—this book is divided into five parts:

1. The Creed, or Principles, of Judaism—the truths and doctrines which the Jewish people are required to believe.

2. The Laws and Observances of Judaism—the laws

ix

which regulate our religious practices and our observance of those days which commemorate important events in the history of our people.

3. The Ethics of Judaism—the moral laws which influence our daily conduct and prescribe our duties to our fellow men.

4. Customs and Symbols of Judaism—the traditional practices in Jewish life and the symbols which are identified with the ritual observances of Judaism.

5. The Sources of Judaism—the books which contain the laws and ceremonies of the Jewish people.

TABLE OF CONTENTS

PAGE

INTRODUCTION ix

PART ONE

THE CREED OF JUDAISM
(Five Principles of Faith)

WHAT THE JEWISH PEOPLE BELIEVE 3
FIRST PRINCIPLE – BELIEF IN GOD 4
   1. The Universal God 6
   2. The Personal God 14
   3. The Ethical God 18
   4. The Unity of God 24
   Our Duties Toward God 27
SECOND PRINCIPLE – BELIEF IN REVELATION ON MT. SINAI 32
THIRD PRINCIPLE – BELIEF IN REWARD AND PUNISHMENT 38
FOURTH PRINCIPLE – BELIEF IN THE IMMORTALITY OF THE
SOUL 42
FIFTH PRINCIPLE – BELIEF IN THE COMING OF THE MES-
SIANIC ERA 49

PART TWO

LAWS AND OBSERVANCES OF JUDAISM

LAWS AND OBSERVANCES OF JUDAISM 57
   1. The Importance of Prayer 59
   2. The Synagogue 61

3. The Jewish Home 65

4. The Sabbath 68

5. The Jewish Calendar 75

6. Rosh Hashanah 77

7. Yom Kippur 84

8. Passover 90

9. Shavuos 98

10. Succos 102

11. Chanukah 107

12. Purim 113

13. Special Days 118

14. Jewish Dietary Laws 121

PART THREE

THE ETHICS OF JUDAISM

OUR DUTIES TO OUR FELLOW MEN 129

1. Humane Ethics 131

2. Social Ethics 136

3. Family Ethics 146

4. Universal Ethics 150

PART FOUR

CUSTOMS AND SYMBOLS OF JUDAISM

CUSTOMS AND SYMBOLS OF JUDAISM 159

1. Customs and Practices in the Synagogue . . . 161

2. Symbols and Religious Objects in the Synagogue 163

3. Symbols and Practices in the Jewish Home . . 167

4. Customs and Symbols of the Sabbath . . . 169

5. Religious Practices in Jewish Life 171

6. Marriage 173
7. Divorce, Agunah, Chalitzah 176
8. Death and Mourning 178

PART FIVE

THE SOURCES OF JUDAISM

1. The Bible 183
   1. Torah (Pentateuch) 184
   2. Neviim (Prophets) 186
   3. Chessuvim (Sacred Writings) 193
2. The Talmud 201
3. The Codes of Jewish Laws 205

BIBLIOGRAPHY 208

GLOSSARY 209

PART ONE

THE CREED OF JUDAISM

The Five Principles of Faith

WHAT THE JEWISH PEOPLE BELIEVE

It is universally conceded that every religion is based on definite beliefs, and Judaism is no exception. It was Maimonides who first summarized the Jewish creed in his "Thirteen Principles of Faith" (Anni Maamin); although the "Beliefs" of Maimonides were challenged by many Jewish scholars, nevertheless, they were generally accepted as the basic principles of Judaism and placed in the "Siddur" to be recited daily at the conclusion of the morning prayers. These thirteen principles were subsequently condensed, by Albo and others, and summarized into five.

"What do the Jewish people believe in?" This question is frequently asked by ourselves and by our neighbors, and though much has been written and spoken on the subject, there are few Jews in America who know the answer. The beliefs of Judaism, based on theological doctrines and on accepted traditions, are the treasured heritage of the House of Israel, but they are seldom taught to the children of Israel. To give a condensed presentation of the five principles of our faith, they are herein summarized as follows: (1) Belief in God; (2) Belief in God's Revelation on Mt. Sinai and in the Holiness of the Bible; (3) Belief in Reward and Punishment; (4) Belief in the Immortality of the Soul; (5) Belief in the Coming of the Messianic Era.

FIRST PRINCIPLE

God is the first and the most enduring foundation upon which Judaism rests. Abraham, the father of the Hebrew group, denounced the practices of idolatry current in his time and pledged himself and his posterity to the service of a single, invisible God. Isaac, Jacob (Israel), and the families of his twelve sons followed the example of Abraham, and the children of Israel became inseparably identified with the God of Israel. In the course of time, the belief in God became the essential element of every religion.

God is known by many names, described in many ways, and compared to many things in creation. His attributes are varied. In the Bible He is described as kind, but also as fearful; as merciful, also as wrathful. When the people of Israel crossed the Red Sea, Moses eulogized God as "a man of war, a hero in battle" (Exodus 15:3). Later on, when the Israelites made the golden calf, Moses appealed to God and described Him, in a series of thirteen attributes, as "merciful, gracious, long-suffering . . ." (Exodus 34:6). Maimonides lists five accepted theories about God as "creeds," and the Cabbalah claims that the fountainhead of God is surrounded by ten descriptive "spheres." These many different descriptions are frequently confusing.

Many books have been written, by Jewish and Christian authors, on the God idea in Judaism. Some of these books contain elaborate elucidations of the spirituality

4

of God; others describe in glowing terms the "Powers" of God which influence man's conduct in life; and still others advance arguments to prove the existence of God. However, a modern approach to this old theme is required. We cannot emphasize one phase of the deity, such as the Ethical, to the neglect of other phases, nor can we dwell exclusively upon the "Oneness" (unity) of God and disregard the many names and titles by which God has been known to the people of Israel. It therefore is necessary, for purposes both of completeness and simplification, to divide our first creed—the Belief in God— into four classifications. We shall endeavor to justify our belief in: (1) The Universal God, (2) The Personal God, (3) The Ethical God, (4) The Unity of God.

1. THE UNIVERSAL GOD

(God in His Relation to the Universe)

A. CREATOR

GOD IS THE CREATOR OF THE WORLD

"In the beginning God created the heavens and the earth" is the first sentence of the Bible. Nothing creates itself. Whether the world was created in six days or in six million years is immaterial. The fact remains that so vast and so perfect a universe could not have come into being without the guiding spirit of a Supreme Creator.

An anecdote tells us that Oliver Cromwell asked Menasseh ben Israel to prove that God was the creator of the world. At that moment a bottle of ink turned over and made several spots on the table and carpet. Menasseh bluntly remarked, "No ink, when spilled at random, will make a good picture, but it will make pictures and designs of all kinds in the hands of an artist. In the same way our beautiful world was not created merely by throwing odd pieces of materials together. It was fashioned by the hands of a divine artist."

"Boreh Olom"—Creator of the World—is the popular name of God used in post-biblical literature. Jewish tradition maintains that the work of creation still continues, and in one of our prayers we recite, "In His goodness, He renews daily the works of creation." Philo says, "As it is the property of fire to burn, and of snow to chill, so it is the property of God to be creating." According to the Talmud, every righteous man who contributes to human

6

happiness and to the progress of the world becomes "a partner of God in the work of creation" (Sabbath 10).

B. RULER

GOD IS THE RULER OF THE UNIVERSE

Left to itself, the world could not exist. Just as the locomotive needs its engineer, the ship its captain, and the business establishment its manager, so the world needs the guiding hand of God. He is the "King" of the world. He coordinates the diverse elements of the universe and makes them function in accordance with established rules.

God is frequently designated in Jewish liturgy as "Melech"—King—and every form of prayer or praise uttered by the Jew contains the words "Melech Ho-olom" —King of the World. Jewish tradition has developed the theory that God is not only the Ruler of the visible world but also of the invisible one, and that His kingdom on earth is only secondary in importance to His kingdom in heaven (Malchus Shomayim). "Adon Olom"—Lord of the Universe—is the most popular hymn of the synagogue, and "Ribbono Shel Olom"—Master of the Universe—is the most popular expression of the Jewish people. Both these phrases testify to our fundamental belief that God is the Ruler of the universe.

In the early days of the Hebrews, the God of Israel was believed to be a local, tribal God. Later, when the children of Israel established their kingdom in Palestine, they came to recognize the God of Israel as their national God. Subsequently, the prophets declared Him the universal God and the Ruler of all mankind—"King over all the earth" (Zech. 14:9).

C. Sustainer

GOD SUSTAINS THE WHOLE OF CREATION

In the early days of religious development people thought that God and nature were inseparably united, and "Naturism," also known as the "Fertility Cult," was the popular religion of the Orient. Rivers, trees, large animals, and all phenomena of nature were worshiped as deities. In biblical days God promised the children of Israel the blessings of rain, dew, and abundant crops as a reward for obedience to His laws and He threatened them with the curses of drought, locusts, and scanty crops as a punishment for disobedience.

In the course of time the "nature" aspect of God declined in importance, but it still plays a part in the religious life of the Jewish people. On the first day of Passover we pray for "Tal" (dew), on Shmini Atzeres we pray for "Geshem" (rain), and in the Grace After Meal we daily thank God "Who feeds and sustains all the creatures of the universe."

D. Omnipotent

GOD IS OMNIPOTENT, HIS POWERS ARE INFINITE

The "Fear of God," a fundamental principle of religion, is based on our conception of God as the "Strong One," as the all-powerful Ruler Who controls the elements of nature, shapes the destinies of nations, and punishes those who disobey His will.

Many violent disturbances of nature, such as earthquakes or floods, are designated as "acts of God." The biblical names of God—El, Shaddai, Godol, Gibbor, Noro, Izuz, Amitz,—describe Him as possessing extraordinary powers. The words of Moses, "Who is like unto Thee, O Lord, among the mighty?" (Ex. 15:11), reverberate daily in our synagogues. The term "Almighty God" is heard not only in the synagogues, but also in churches and in daily conversation. All these terms and expressions testify to our belief in the omnipotence of God.

Judaism also requires us to believe that God can perform miracles. Through Moses, the miracle man of the wilderness, and Elisha, the miracle man of the prophetic guild, the unlimited powers of the Almighty were manifested. True religion and faith in God are complete only when they include faith in miracles. Daily, when wealth and power are of no avail, man seeks aid from God. When the physicians cannot save a man, we pray to God for his life and expect a miracle to happen. When life is endangered by fire or water, we instinctively pray for God's intervention and again express our faith in miracles. We, the people of Israel, may ascribe our very existence to a series of miracles performed in our behalf by Him Who is the eternal "Guardian of Israel."

Many people have argued the case of miracles, claiming that the laws of nature are fixed and not subject to change. In reply we may say, first of all, that *we do not know* the laws of nature. Present-day scientists speak of the gross ignorance of the scientists of the past, and it is reasonable to assume that the scientists of coming generations will ridicule the platitudes of the scientists of today. Secondly, the laws of nature *are not fixed* at all. What was considered impossible one thousand years ago, because of the "fixed" laws of nature, is possible today. An airplane and a radio would have been "miracles" in the days of the Revolution; now they function with clearly defined natural laws. Our belief in God as the Creator therefore requires that we recognize His ability to interfere with the normal operations of the world and to change, if He so desires, the natural laws of creation.

E. Omniscient

GOD IS OMNISCIENT, HE KNOWS EVERYTHING

God knows the mysteries as well as the revealed things in life. An oriental anecdote tells us that a man once asked his friend to perform a heinous crime, adding, "Nobody sees us." To this his friend replied, "But God sees us." The thief or traitor who commits a sin under the cover of darkness fails to realize that God sees his foul deed. It is in keeping with the belief in God's omniscience that the Talmud classifies the thief as a greater sinner than the highway robber, for the latter fears neither God nor man, while the former fears man and does not fear God and so places man above God. Sin and the temptation of sin are frequently overcome when man knows that God knows.

F. Omnipresent

GOD IS OMNIPRESENT; HE IS EVERYWHERE

Whenever we think of the universal presence of God we are reminded of the words of the first Isaiah, "The whole earth is full of His glory" (Is. 6:3), or of the words of the second Isaiah, "The heaven is His throne and the earth His footstool" (Is. 66:1). In the Talmud God is often called "Hamokom" (The Place), for "as space— Mokom—encompasses all things, so does God encompass the world instead of being encompassed by it" (Gen. Rabba 68:9).

To the question, "Where is God?" Bachya replied,
"He is nearer than all things near from the standpoint of
His acts, but farther than all things far from the standpoint of His essential glory and likeness." Judah Halevy
said, "Lord, where shall I find Thee? Exalted and secret
is Thy place; where shall I not find Thee? The world is
full of Thy glory."

A Roman general once said to Rabbi Judah, the editor
of the Mishnah, "Tell me, where is God?" to which Rabbi
Judah replied, "Tell me, where is *not* God?" Man can-
not run away from himself, nor can he escape the presence of God. Adam could not hide from the presence of
God; Jonah's life was imperiled when he tried to escape
God's presence. As the Psalmist says, "Where shall I go
from Thy spirit, where shall I flee from Thy presence?"
(Ps. 139:7). There is not a remote corner in this universe
which is not permeated by the presence of God. By the
Jew, especially, God's presence is invariably felt, as the
Talmud remarks, "When the Jew leaves the Holy land
and goes into exile, the Shechinah, God's presence, goes
with him" (Megillah 29).

G. SPIRITUAL

GOD IS INCORPOREAL; HE IS SPIRITUAL, NOT MATERIAL

God is a universal, spiritual power which resembles
nothing of material form. As Maimonides puts it in the
Anni Maamin, "I believe . . . that He is not a physical
body, that corporeal relations do not apply to Him, and
that there exists nothing that is in any way similar to
Him."

In ancient mythology gods had bodily forms and were
subject to physical weaknesses, but not so in Israel, and

while pagan gods were glorified by statues, ikons, and images, our people adhered to the second of the ten commandments which said, "Thou shalt not make unto thyself any graven image, nor any likeness of anything that is in heaven above, or on the earth beneath, or in the water under the earth."

A Roman emperor once said to a Jewish sage, "Show me your God; I want to see him." To which the Rabbi replied, "The sun in heaven is but a messenger of God, an insignificant part of His glory, yet you cannot look at it with the naked eye. How can you expect to see God Himself?"

God is a divine spirit. The people of Israel could never worship idols because they could not create an image of their God. The Talmud speaks apologetically of the fact that the Torah spoke "in the language of man," picturing God in human likeness, possessing hands, feet, eyes, etc., and subjecting Him to human emotions, such as wrath, vengeance, jealousy, etc. This, the Talmud declares, was done in order to make the God-idea accessible to people whose sphere of comprehension was limited.

H. Eternal

GOD IS ETERNAL; HE WAS, IS, AND EVER WILL BE

God is known by many Hebrew names, but the name that is most quoted in the Bible is "Yahveh" which is generally interpreted as meaning "the ever present One." Some commentators claim that Yahveh is a composite noun derived from the words *Hoyo, Hoveh, Yiheye*— "was, is, will be." Maimonides summarizes the eternity of God in these words, "He was the first, He will be the last." The names "Rock," and "Rock of Ages," are symbolic of His unmoved stability. Everything in the world is changeable; He alone is permanent. He is the God of our fathers, the God of history. He is above time and space. "From everlasting to everlasting Thou art God" (Ps. 90:2).

2. THE PERSONAL GOD

(God's Spiritual Personality)

A. A Divine "Personality" Dominates the Universe

Early biblical records indicate that our ancestors were accustomed to think of the deity as personal. God walked on earth; He revealed His glory to man; He spoke with and through the prophets. In the course of time Judaism has developed many aspects of the God-idea, but retained the original belief in a personal God.

There are many definitions of the words "person" and "personality." We often think that personality must be associated with a physical body, but experience makes it clear that a person is not only a body. If he were, our persons would become large when we grow stout and small when we become thin. A body may be mutilated by amputation, yet the ego, or self, remains intact. On the other hand, the body may remain intact in death, yet the person is gone. The body is simply the instrument through which a person, or a soul, expresses itself. A person is a self-conscious being capable of thought and self-control. This ability to think causes him to act in accordance with his thoughts, to formulate plans, and to seek definite ends. The magnitude of his "personality" is determined by the mental and spiritual qualifications which constitute him as a "person."

Now, take the case of God and the universe. There are thought and direction in the daily processes of the world,

14

and the powers which control and dominate the universe
constitute the spiritual "Personality" of God. For if God
did not possess the characteristics which make for personality, then, man would be greater than the power
which created him. It is therefore reasonable to state that
man is endowed with "personality" because his soul is a
small part of God Who is the all-embracing, universal
"Personality."

B. The Personal Pronouns "I" and "Thou"

God often uses the personal pronoun when He speaks
of Himself as "Anni Adonoi"—I am the Lord. Nahum
Sokolov once stated that the term "Anni" does not always
stand for the individual ego but frequently expresses the
"Anni Hakibutzi," the collective personality. When used
by God, the word "Anni" indicates the vast Personality
of the universe.

In most of his prayers, the Jew speaks directly to God
with the words "Boruch Attoh"—"Blessed art Thou"
or "Praised be Thou." The word *Attoh* ("Thou" or
"You") suggests the thought that the Jew addresses himself to a personality. All the prayers uttered by man, in
the synagogue and in the church, are addressed to a personal God in whatever form He may be conceived. This
theory always prevailed in Judaism, and historic records
indicate that the reason why Spinoza was excommunicated from the synagogue was largely due to his refusal
to subscribe to the Jewish belief in a personal God.

In the "Adon Olom" hymn the Jew sings "V'hu Eli"—
He is *my* God. While philosophy may prove, or disprove,
the existence of a supernatural deity, religion advances
the theory of a personal God and causes man to exclaim,
"He is *my* God!"

C. God as a Companion

The "companionship" of God is religion's greatest gift to man. With God as a companion and friend, man's life becomes fuller, richer, nobler. The biblical quotation, "Man does not live by bread alone," may be paraphrased as, "Man cannot go through life alone." He needs social intercourse and human friendship, and he also needs divine companionship. We like to share our joys as well as our sorrows, and it is a source of comfort to us when we share our experiences with God, the confident friend in Whom we can trust.

Man's conscience, the "still small voice" that speaks within, reveals the presence of God within the soul of man. Morris Joseph defines the conscience as "God's most intimate presence in the soul of man." The belief in God as a companion has always inspired man and helped him to endure the vicissitudes of life. It has heartened men and women to defy the grim realities of misery and death with such religious expressions as "The Lord is with me, I fear not," or "Even though I walk through the valley of the shadow of death, I fear no evil, for Thou art with me." In his life the Jew has always cherished the companionship of God, calling Him "my rock," "my refuge," "my eternal strength," "my redeemer." The tragic history of the people of Israel is testimony that through the ages the Jew has endured the agonies of martyrdom with the knowledge that God is his companion even unto death.

D. God as a Father

We speak of God as the Father of all mankind and frequently address our petitions to "Our Heavenly Father."

The term "Father," like the word "Attoh," suggests a personal God to whom we appeal for aid.

We speak of God as "father" and not as "mother," or as "brother," because human society has largely been worked out along patriarchal lines. God was originally conceived as the leader of the universal household, as the father who not only grants his children love and tenderness but also gives them strength, leadership, and protection. The "Fatherhood of God" expresses best the universal personality of the Creator.

In the early days of the Bible, God was designated as the father and Israel as the son. Moses said to Pharaoh, "Thus saith the Lord; 'my son, my first born, is Israel'" (Ex. 4:22). Speaking to the children of Israel, Moses said, "As a father chastiseth his son, so does the Lord, your God, chastise you" (Deut. 8:5). The prophets spoke repeatedly of God's paternal attitude toward Israel; but Malachi, the last of the prophets, expressed the idea of the universal Fatherhood of God when he said, "Have we not all one Father? Hath not one God created us?" (Mal. 2:10).

In the period of the second century C. E., the officiating priests (Cohanim) used the word "Father" (Abba) in public worship. In the days of the Talmud most of the prayers of the synagogue began with the words "Ovinu Shebashomayim"—Our Father in Heaven—but later on we adopted the now popular form "Ovinu Malkeinu"—Our Father, Our King. For a modern interpretation of the word "Father" we quote Kaufmann Kohler, "In Judaism, God is conceived as a loving Father who purposes to lead His children to happiness and salvation."

3. THE ETHICAL GOD

(God as an Example to Humanity)

A. ETHICAL MONOTHEISM

The most rational approach to the God-idea is from the ethical viewpoint. We often hear such expressions as "God is One and humanity is one," "God is love," "God is justice," "God is truth." These theories are summarized as "ethical monotheism" and are of incalculable value in presenting the finer aspects of the God-idea. People of limited faith who hesitate to go the full length of Jewish theology are especially captivated by these theories which place God as the ideal of all morality and goodness. Another doctrine has recently been expounded in which God is presented as the motivating "Power" that makes for justice, for kindness, for love. This theory is based on a Talmudic quotation, "Ye shall cleave to the Lord, your God, by emulating His deeds; as He is merciful, so be ye merciful; as He is kind and patient, so be ye kind and patient" (Sabbath 133).

B. SOURCE OF HOLINESS

"Holy, Holy, Holy, is the Lord of hosts" was the exultant expression of Isaiah when he first beheld the glory of God. He subsequently referred to the Lord as the "K'dosh Yisroel,"—the holy one of Israel. It is the task of religion to elevate man to a state of holiness and thus confirm the eternal truth that man was created in the image of God. "Kiddush Hashem" (literally the sanctifi-

cation of God's name) is the Jewish term for martyrdom;
it is based on the premise that every Jew should be ready
to offer his very life in order to prove the theory of the
"Holiness" of God and of His name. The most popular
name of God, as used in post-biblical literature, is "Hako-
dosh Boruch Hu"—the Holy One, blessed be He. Moses
announced the most essential prerequisite of religion
when he said, in the name of God, "Ye shall be holy, for
I, the Lord your God, am holy" (Lev. 19:2).

C. PERFECTION

"Thou shalt be perfect (Tomim) before the Lord, thy
God" (Deut. 18:13) is one of the most significant quotations of the Bible. The word "Tomim" is frequently used
to describe the ideal type of man. It is true that the temptations of life are many and that man may not always
succeed in reaching a state of perfection, yet it is his
bounden duty to aim toward that goal. Man feels intuitively that an Ethical God, the ideal of perfection,
desires His children to live in accordance with the ethical
laws of religion. Man's striving to imitate God and to
achieve a state of perfection constitutes the history of
mankind as well as the history of religion.

D. JUSTICE AND TRUTH

God created order out of chaos. He established laws
for the course of nature, and He also laid down laws to
regulate daily intercourse among the children of His
creation. Adherence to the latter laws we call "Justice,"
and God, the supreme Judge of the universe, is recognized as the ideal of justice. Abraham, the first Hebrew,
was the first one to exploit the theory of justice when he
pleaded the cause of the people of Sodom with the perti-

nent question, "Wilt Thou, the Judge of the universe, not do justice?" (Gen. 18:25).

"God is just in all His ways" (Ps. 145:17), is recited daily by the observant Jew. The admonition, "Justice, justice shalt thou pursue" (Deut. 16:20), is taken seriously by the Jewish people, and a truly godly man is called in Hebrew a "Tzadik," which literally means "a man of justice." We believe that God is just in meting out punishment, even though His ways are incomprehensible to the limited vision of man. When faced with the grim reality of death, or when informed of the death of a person, the Jew accepts the verdict of God with pious resignation and exclaims, "Blessed art Thou, the true Judge."

Judaism, though often designated as "a religion of law," does not consider the practice of justice merely from the legal standpoint, but from the human standpoint as well. Even charity, the manifestation of man's humane attitude to his fellow man, is characterized in Hebrew as "Tzdokoh"—an "act of justice." To the prophet Amos, God *is* justice. Isaiah's ideal of religion is proclaimed in the words, "Keep ye justice, and do righteousness, for My salvation is near to come" (Is. 56:1). The Psalmist aptly says, "Justice and righteousness are the foundations of Thy throne" (Ps. 89:15).

Since justice and truth are inseparable elements in the moral order of the universe, the Jew also seeks and finds in God the symbol of truth. Malice and falsehood usually accompany every act of injustice. It has therefore been accepted in Judaism that the God of justice is also the God of truth. "In Thy hands I trust my soul, Thou wilt redeem me, for Thou art a God of Truth" (Ps. 31:6).

God is truth. He desires naught but truth, and therefore hypocrisy in every form, even in the service of religion, is loathsome to Him. Isaiah, in the first chapter of his book, expresses this idea conclusively. Jeremiah exclaims "Israel's God is the God of truth, the living God and everlasting King" (Jer. 10:10). A Talmudic saying is: "Truth is the seal of God" (Sabbath 55).

E. MERCY AND LOVE

The Ethical God is conceived as the divine symbol of such ethical virtues as mercy, love, and kindness. As an advocate of justice, He may be described as a "God of Wrath," but as the loving Father of all humanity, He is known as a "God of Mercy." "He loveth righteousness and justice, the earth is full of the loving kindness of the Lord" (Ps. 33:5). In his daily prayers and on all festive occasions the Jew is told to "give thanks unto the Lord, for He is good; His mercy endureth forever" (Ps. 136:1).

Judaism teaches that justice and mercy are not two separate powers in the Deity. They are the two sides of the same divine Power. Justice forms the basis of human morality, but its sternness is lessened by the milder elements of kindness and mercy. The sages of the Talmud therefore say, "When the Creator saw that man could not endure, if measured by the standard of strict justice, He joined His attribute of mercy to that of justice and created man by the combined principle of both" (Gen. Rabba 8:4).

The command "Thou shalt love the Lord, thy God" is known to every Jew, who is told to "love Him because He loves you." When Moses pleaded for his people and uttered the famous attributes of God, he placed mercy as the first one. . . . "The Lord, the Lord, is a merciful and gracious God" (Ex. 34:6). To the prophet Hosea God *is* love.

God's merciful attitude toward the sinner is a salient feature of Judaism. We are repeatedly told that the person who confesses his sins and repents of his evil ways will be forgiven. Our belief that God pardons and graciously receives the penitent sinner is especially substantiated in the ceremonies, prayers, and symbols of Yom Kippur. On that day we reiterate in our liturgy, "God hath no delight in the death of the sinner, but that he shall return from his ways and live" (Ez. 33:11). The experiences of Jonah, as read in the synagogue on Yom Kippur, testify to God's eagerness to pardon the iniquities of His children.

The question has frequently been asked, "If God is our merciful Father, why is there so much suffering in the world?" The answer is that in the scheme of the universe it is often necessary to have the forces of evil function simultaneously with the forces of good so that man may learn to appreciate the good in comparison with the evil. In the case of the Jew it may well be said that he has learned from experience to retain a spirit of optimism and to see the hand of a merciful God even in times of adversity. "Even in wrath He remembereth mercy" (Habak. 3:3). It is significant that in our Grace after Meals we, the people who were the foremost victims of merciless atrocities, thank God for life and for the blessings of life with a series of prayers in which we present our petitions to "Horachamon"—the "Merciful One."

Man is born with an evil "Yetzer" and with selfish inclinations. Kindness and mercy are *not* natural human traits, but they become so when man, influenced by religion, seeks to imitate the ways of a merciful God. It is

significant that the barbaric pagans of today seek to suppress the Judeao-Christian theory of "mercy" because
they believe that it is conducive to weakness. We, the
people of Israel, know that the divine attribute of mercy
is one of the foundations upon which humanity rests and
that this attribute of God, to be emulated by man, was
first proclaimed by Israel, then copied by the monotheistic religions, and subsequently accepted by the world.

4. THE UNITY OF GOD

(Addonoi Echod)

A. THE THEORY OF MONOTHEISM

The "Unity" of God is the first and foremost belief of the Jewish people; our eternal slogan is, "Hear O Israel, the Lord is our God, the Lord is *One*." In ancient times people practiced polytheism, the religion of many gods. There was a deity assigned to every element or phenomenon of nature, and every human emotion, good or bad, and every human act, constructive or destructive, was thought to be controlled by a different god. In place of hundreds of rival idols, the people of Israel gave to mankind the theory of monotheism, the religion of one God. The "Unity" of God thus means that the powers of the world and the elements of nature are all united in One God.

The monotheistic idea has often been singled out as Israel's foremost contribution to the religious development of man, as the theory which brings harmony into the intellectual and moral world. The word "Elohim" (literally Gods) which appears frequently in biblical narratives has been interpreted in the Talmud to mean "the many creative elements that are united in One." The biblical expression, "and God said, 'Let us create man,'" is generally interpreted as the divine expression of the collective "We," a term used by kings, judges, preachers, and editorial writers.

Ibn Gabirol in his "Crown of Royalty" puts the sub-

lime idea of monotheism into poetic form: "One art
Thou; wise men wonder at the mystery of Thy unity, not
knowing what it is. One art Thou; not like the one of
dimension or number, as neither addition nor change,
neither attribute nor quality affect Thy being. Thou art
God, who sustainest all beings by Thy divinity, who hold-
est all creatures in Thy unity. Thou art God, and there
is no distinction between Thy unity, Thy eternity, and
Thy being. All is mystery and however the names may
differ, they all tell that Thou art but one."

B. "UNITY" IN JUDAISM

Judaism has no pantheon of pagan idols, no deities or
heroes in the skies, or on earth, or in the seas. "I am the
Lord, and besides me there is no God" (Is. 45:21). Christianity denounced the Greek and Roman mythology and
accepted the unity of God, but in the course of time this
"unity" became a "trinity." Islam accepted the theory of
the unity of God, but added to it the belief in Mohammed, Allah's "messenger." The Jewish people, rigorously monotheistic in their faith, have never worshiped
a human being as a deity. They even preferred to have the
grave of Moses remain unknown, lest it be turned into
a sacred shrine and the great lawgiver be indirectly
idolized.

Judaism is opposed to the dualism of Zoroaster which
divides the world into two rival realms of good and evil;
it is also opposed to the idea of an intermediary between
man and his Maker. Judaism maintains that God is om-
nipotent; that He must be alone. One of the creeds of
Maimonides is, "I believe . . . that He is a Unity, and
that there is no Oneness like His in any way and that
He alone is our God; He was, He is, and He will be."

C. "Unity" and the People of Israel

The belief in the Unity of God runs parallel with the history of Israel. The theory of the Unity of God was originated, according to tradition, by Abraham, the first Hebrew. It was later proclaimed on Mt. Sinai in the command, "Thou shalt have no other gods before Me." It was the basic theory in the legislation of Moses, the all-pervading motive in the preachings of the prophets, and the fundamental principle in the development of Judaism. Our people were constantly reminded that the words, "Hear, O Israel, the Lord is our God, the Lord is One" are the slogan of our faith and that these words were not only to be deeply rooted in our hearts, but also to be written "upon the doorposts of thy house and upon thy gates." Through the ages the "Unity" idea (Adonoi Echod) was loudly proclaimed and heroically defended by the Jewish people. When the Jew faced the agonies of martyrdom, he pronounced the "Sh'ma Yisroel" and died with the words "Adonoi Echod" on his lips.

The Unity of God also suggests the existence of an allegorical unity between God, Israel, and the Torah. The Talmud maintains that "God, Israel, and the Torah are united and inseparable." In this connection it may be stated that the Jewish people, scattered as they are throughout the earth, may disagree on matters of religious opinion, and yet they all agree upon the importance of the words "Adonoi Echod." They may have different prayers and different views on Judaism, but they all have the same "Sh'ma Yisroel." The Unity of God is the universal idea which tends to unite the people of Israel in all parts of the world.

OUR DUTIES TOWARD GOD

Judaism contains a number of commandments which specify our duties toward God. They are "Thou shalt love the Lord, thy God," "Thou shalt fear the Lord, thy God," "Serve the Lord," etc. These admonitions are religious duties, indispensable in the manifestation of our belief in God. We therefore place the chapter on "Duties" in this part of the book because they are the direct corollary of our allegiance to the first creed—Belief in God. Our duties toward God call for the following:

1. FAITH

The first prerequisite for a religious life is faith in God, and this is why the word "Faith" is another name for religion. The prophet Habakkuk aptly summarizes the whole of religion in one sentence, "The righteous shall live by his faith" (Habak. 2:4). Each individual must have implicit faith in God. Even when misfortune comes and God's ways seem beyond our comprehension, we must not abandon faith in a just and merciful Father. Job, the tragic figure of the Bible, exclaimed, amidst excruciating pains, "Even though He slay me, I shall still have faith in Him" (Job 13:15). Each one of the thirteen creeds of Judaism, as formulated by Maimonides, begins with the words, "I believe with perfect faith . . ."

2. FEAR

Religion imposes upon us a special duty, the fear of God. "The beginning of wisdom is the fear of God"

(Ps. 111:10). Man obeys the laws of the land because he
fears the powers of man; he must also fear the infinitely
greater powers of God. Jochanan ben Zakai admonished
his disciples to "Fear God as you fear man."

Fear is often the source of evil, but it is also the cause
of many blessings. Many human attitudes that are bene-
ficial to life and progress, such as caution, ambition, and
foresight have their origin in fear. The word "respect" is
interpreted in Hebrew as "Yiras Hakovod," a combination of honor and fear. To show our proper respect to
God, our Heavenly Father, we must honor Him and fear
Him. It is interesting to observe that throughout our
biblical literature, religion is invariably spoken of as
"The fear of God."

3. Love

"Thou shalt love the Lord, thy God, with all thy heart,
with all thy soul, and with all thy might" (Deut. 6:5).
These words are familiar to every Jew in every part of the
world. God is our loving Father, our creator, our protector, the "Guardian of Israel Who neither slumbereth
nor sleepeth" (Ps. 121:4). The prophet Hosea, through
his own example, intimated that "God is Love." The
Talmud admonishes us that we are to love God whether
he deals kindly with us or not.

4. Holiness

"Ye shall be holy, for I, the Lord your God, am holy"
(Lev. 19:2). This quotation is one of the fundamental
doctrines of Judaism. Man is composed of two elements,
human and divine. Religion primarily urges man to sub-
jugate the human passions within him and to heed the
divine call of his soul. God, the "Holy One of Israel," is

the embodiment of justice, mercy, and love; it is the duty
of the Jew to follow the ways of God and to strive toward
perfection and holiness. "Worship the Lord in the beauty
of Holiness" (Ps. 29:2).

5. WORSHIP

Man inherently tends to worship a superior being. The
pagans of old have worshiped the elements of nature
and the national heroes who became legendary deities;
unlike them, the Jew has assumed a self-imposed duty to
worship his God. Prayer is the link which unites man
with his creator. To make prayer complete it must be
accompanied by a sacrifice, in one form or another.
Prayer and sacrifice were combined in the Tabernacle, in
the wilderness, and in the Temple at Jerusalem and
prayer and sacrifice (religion and charity) will always constitute the foundations of Judaism. Prayer is not merely
the act of asking for something, it comprises such things
as praise, reverence, humility, gratitude, and petition.
The admonition to serve the Lord "with all thy heart"
means to serve Him through prayer, the expression of the
heart.

6. KNOWLEDGE

"In all thy ways, know Him" (Prov. 3:6). Judaism imposes upon us a special duty to "know" God. King David,
in his last words to Solomon, said, "Know the Lord, thy
God, and serve Him" (Ch. 1, 28:9). The admonition,
"Thou shalt teach the words of God unto thy children,"
has always been rigidly observed in Jewish life.

There are religions which prefer to keep their followers in ignorance and hold out to them the promise of
that divine bliss which comes with blind faith, but Ju-

daism maintains that ignorance and piety are incompatible. Whenever and wherever there is a decline in loyalty to Judaism, it is almost invariably caused by a lack of knowledge of things Jewish. Many a devout Jew would rather "learn Torah" than recite his daily prayers, for in Judaism the study of the Torah, or of the Talmud, is considered a religious act in itself. In order to live a godly life the Jew must assume the special duty of knowing God through the study of the Torah.

7. OBEDIENCE

Obedience to the laws of God is the fundamental principle of religion. The commandments and ordinances of God, as contained in the Bible, modified in the Talmud, and codified in the Shulchan Aruch, form the pillars upon which the structure of Judaism rests. Judaism asserts that the laws of the Torah were never abrogated. Time and conditions may change, the observance of Jewish laws may become increasingly difficult, but the laws themselves will never become obsolete. Every noble deed performed by the Jew is described as a "Mitzvah," an act performed in obedience to the laws of God.

8. GRATITUDE

"Give thanks unto the Lord, for He is good; His mercy endureth forever" (Ps. 118:1). Gratitude is an essential factor in man's life, but while gratitude to man is limited in its scope and is based upon narrow considerations, our gratitude to God knows no bounds. It is our duty to be thankful to God for the bounties of nature, for life, and for all things that come to us, good or bad. To quote the words of Job, "Shall we receive only the good things from the hands of God and not the evil ones?" (Job 2:10).

Those people who thank God for success and happiness but rebel against Him in times of adversity are usually without a truly religious spirit. Our ritual contains a series of "Brochos," expressions of thanks to God, for everything that sustains life and for every occurrence that lends interest to our earthly existence.

9. HUMILITY

"What is man that Thou thinkest of him?" (Ps. 8:5). The answer that frequently comes to us is, "dust thou art and unto dust thou shalt return"; to be meek and humble before God is the duty of every Jew.

When we recite the words, "Thine, O Lord, are the greatness, the power, the glory, the victory, and the majesty" (Ch. 1:29:11), we cannot but feel humble and insignificant before Him. To quote the prophet Micah, "What does the Lord require of thee? Only to do justice, to love mercy, and to walk humbly with thy God" (Micah 6:8).

SECOND PRINCIPLE

BELIEF IN GOD'S REVELATION ON MT. SINAI AND IN THE HOLINESS OF THE BIBLE

(This chapter is divided into four sections)

1. We Believe That the Ten Commandments Were Given to Israel on Mt. Sinai by Divine Revelation

We, the Jewish people, obey many religious laws, and the reason for our observance of these laws is our belief in their divine origin. Without this belief in "Revelation" and in the divinely inspired laws of the Torah, the very foundations of the structure of Judaism would crumble and disappear. We constantly refer to the commandments of the Torah as the Law of God. "The law of the Lord is perfect, restoring the soul" (Ps. 19:8).

2. We Believe in the Sanctity of the Bible

The Bible is the primary source of the laws of morality which God revealed to Israel through Moses and through His prophets. The Jewish Bible, the Old Testament, was not written to extol a certain theory or to glorify an individual. In fact, it was not even intended to be a book of religion, but a book of life and, like life itself, its contents vary in character. In it, accounts of human failings are recorded side by side with sublime deeds of holiness. To the Jew, religion is life, and the Bible is his book of life.

It is commonly believed that the Bible was written by

man under the inspiration of God. There have always been disputes as to whether or not each letter of the Bible was inspired, but those eternal arguments do not deter us from our belief in the inspiration of the Bible as a whole.

3. WE BELIEVE THAT THE PROPHETS WERE DIVINELY INSPIRED WHEN THEY SAID, "THUS SAITH THE LORD"

"Prophecy" is the message of God sent to the people, and the bringer of that message is called a prophet. The belief in God is inadequate unless we believe in what He said and in the rules and laws which He laid down for our guidance. We therefore believe that God has communicated with men and revealed His nature and His laws to them. "For the Lord, God, will do nothing but He revealeth His counsel to His servants, the prophets" (Amos 3:7).

In the early days of its history, Israel had, in common with other nations, kings, warriors, statesmen, poets, musicians, etc.; but Israel gave to the world that type of man which no other nation produced:—Prophets, "God-intoxicated" visionaries.

4. WE BELIEVE THAT WHEN THE JEWISH PEOPLE WERE GIVEN THE TEN COMMANDMENTS, THEY WERE DESIGNATED TO BE THE "CHOSEN PEOPLE"

There are three theories of Israel's place as the chosen people; they are as follows:

(a) CHOSEN FOR GLORY

Orthodox Judaism, as well as Orthodox Christianity, adheres to the literal interpretation of the biblical statement that the children of Israel were chosen to be different and distinctive. This interpretation was always a source of pride to the synagogue and a source of envy to the church.

Jewish liturgy constantly refers to the term, "Thou hast chosen us from all the people." The Kiddush prayer, on Sabbath and on holidays, tells the proud position of the Jew as the chosen of God, and when the Jew is called up to the Torah, he offers thanks to God, "Asher Bochar Bonu . . . ," "Who chose us from all the people and gave us the Torah." At no time, however, did the Jew think himself chosen because of his racial superiority. Intermarriage between Jew and Gentile was frowned upon by the synagogue on grounds of religious and social, rather than racial, incompatibility.

The Christian church has frequently interpreted the "chosen people" theory to mean that the Jewish people claim racial and moral superiority and the right to dominate the Christian world, and even such liberals as G. B. Shaw and H. G. Wells cling to these traditional misconceptions. Said G. B. Shaw: "The fault of the Jew is his enormous arrogance based on his claim to belong to God's chosen race." To quote H. G. Wells: "The Jewish people are haunted by a persuasion that they are a chosen people with distinctive privileges over their Gentile fellow creatures."

(b) CHOSEN FOR SERVICE

Another theory maintains that the children of Israel were "called," or "conscripted" to spread throughout the world the knowledge of God and to assume responsibilities as the servants of the Lord. The prophet Amos was the first to advance this theory when he said, "Ye only have I known of all the families of the earth, therefore

will I punish you for all your iniquities" (Amos 3:2). The
fifty-third chapter of Isaiah speaks of the Jew as God's
suffering servant. Many of the prophets imply that the
Jewish people, through their historic heritage, have assumed a self-imposed duty to be better, more just, more
ethical, and more God-like than the heathens.

(C) CHOSEN FOR A MISSION

Reform Judaism has evolved a theory that the people
of Israel were chosen to perform eternally the mission of
bringing religion to humanity. This theory claims that
the Jewish people, having been chosen for a special mission, have promulgated the teachings of monotheism and
have thus raised the status of humanity to a higher level.
This theory further claims that the Jewish people were
miraculously preserved through the ages so that they
might serve as the living witnesses of the eternal powers
of God. According to this interpretation, the dispersion
of the Jewish people through the ages was not intended
by God as a punishment to Israel, but as a service to
humanity.

NOTES ON REVELATION

(For Advanced Students and Adult Study Groups)

Jewish tradition has it that even though it is recorded
in the Bible that the children of Israel were chosen to
receive the Ten Commandments on Mt. Sinai, yet the
Revelation was intended for the whole of mankind. The
Talmud tells us that God spoke to Moses in seventy languages, the number of languages that were then known
to the world.

The frequent disputes about the technical process of the Revelation do not offset our belief in its validity, just as the dispute concerning the time element in the creation of the world does not dislodge our belief in God as the Creator of the universe.

Tradition has it that many of the nations of antiquity refused to accept the Torah, but the children of Israel received God's commandments with the exclamation, "We shall do and obey."

Judah Halevy, an extremist on the "chosen people" theory, states in his "Kuzari," that "Israel is the heart of the nations."

In commenting on Revelation, the extreme rabbinical view is that every letter of the Torah was written by Moses at the dictation of God; this theory is called "Torah min hashomayim"—"The Torah is from Heaven."

The term "Holy Writ" is often taken literally in Jewish life, and even the parchment upon which the Torah is written is considered holy.

The Jewish people always believed in the inspiration of the Bible, yet they were never fundamentalists in the strict sense of the word. The fact that we strenuously rejected the fundamentalist theories of the Karaites and accepted the interpretations of the Talmud on all matters of biblical legalism indicates our belief in the flexibility of the word of God.

Tradition has it that the doctrines of the Talmud, or the "Oral Law," were also "revealed unto Moses on Mt. Sinai."

Describing the importance of Torah to the people of Israel, Saadia Gaon said, "Our nation is only a nation by reason of its Torah."

It is difficult to translate or to define the meaning of

the word "Torah." It is usually referred to as the "Five Books of Moses," or "Pentateuch," or "Law," but to the Jew that word stands for religion, morality, nationhood, culture, ethics. In short, it is a divine Constitution regulating the way of life of the Jewish people.

THIRD PRINCIPLE

BELIEF IN REWARD AND PUNISHMENT

(Divided into four sections)

1. WE BELIEVE THAT THE LAW OF REWARD AND PUNISHMENT IS THE NATURAL LAW OF THE UNIVERSE

Every act of man is subjected to the law of reward and punishment. The laws of society regulating our daily life hold out many promises and threats. The laws of the nation, safeguarding life and property through regulations, are intended to encourage or to restrain the citizen in what he does. Religion was designed to improve life and to make it more significant. Therefore it is obvious that religion, like life itself, should be controlled by the inevitable laws of the universe.

2. WE BELIEVE THAT MAN WAS ENDOWED WITH THE ABILITY TO "CHOOSE" HIS MODE OF LIFE (B'CHIRAH) AND TO DO EITHER GOOD OR EVIL

In advancing the theory of "freedom of will," Judaism stresses the importance of the word, "B'chirah," which signifies man's ability to fashion his own life and to do either good or evil. According to this theory, the righteous man cannot say, "I deserve no credit for my good deeds, for I was born with noble inclinations"; nor can the wicked man say, "I should not be punished for my evil deeds, for my sins are due to heredity or to an evil environment." Judaism maintains that every individual is personally responsible for his deeds. It further maintains that a man cannot escape responsibility for his deeds by blaming them on others. Heredity, environment, and other circumstances may be contributing factors in man's life, but man has the ability to overcome many of the obstacles in his path. "Man can become an angel; he can also become a devil" (Schiller).

3. WE BELIEVE THAT, DIRECTLY OR INDIRECTLY, VIRTUE IS REWARDED AND SIN PUNISHED

The function of religion is to teach mankind what is right and what is wrong. Religion not only admonishes us to do good and to avoid sin, but it also emphasizes the fact that virtue (Hebrew, "Mitzvah") is rewarded and sin (Hebrew, "Averah") punished.

The Bible promises many rewards for acts of righteousness and threatens dire punishment for deeds of wickedness (Lev. & Deut.). These admonitions were originally directed to the nation as a whole, but in the course of time they have been accepted as applicable to the individual as well. They stress the point that man's supreme duty is to realize that he was created in the image of God.

Judaism tells us that God is holy and perfect and that He wants man to be likewise. Therefore, every immoral or evil deed is a sin because it is contrary to the will of God. A person who disobeys the laws of God is guilty of sin; a person who disregards the traditions of his people is guilty of sin; a person who is intemperate or indulges in physical excesses, undermining the health of his body which was intended to be of service to God and man, is guilty of sin.

Rewards and punishments vary in accordance with mental attitudes, places, and circumstances. What is reward or punishment to one person is meaningless to another. A guilty conscience is often sufficient punishment for sins committed, while a state of happiness and contentment may be ample reward for good deeds. Public opinion, favorable or unfavorable, is frequently the most effective medium for reward or punishment. Often too, in the words of the Jewish sages, "the reward of a noble deed is the noble deed itself, and the punishment of sin is the sin itself" (Pirke Aboth 4:2).

4. WE RETAIN OUR FAITH IN THE TRADITIONAL BELIEF THAT THE HUMAN SOUL, AFTER DEATH, WILL BE REWARDED OR PUNISHED IN ACCORDANCE WITH DEEDS COMMITTED

From time immemorial people have asked, "Why do the righteous suffer?" or "Why do the wicked prosper?" Judaism answers these questions by maintaining that the real reward and punishment will be in the world to come. "Know ye that the reward of the righteous is in the world to come" (Pirke Aboth 2:21). According to this theory, the righteous man who suffers in this world will be amply rewarded in the hereafter, while the wicked man who enjoys the pleasures of this world will be doomed to perdition in the world to come.

NOTES ON REWARD AND PUNISHMENT

(For Advanced Students and Adult Study Groups)

Judaism believes in the presence of evil in this world but denies that humanity is corrupted and that the world is tainted with sin. Judaism believes that sin in the world is the exception, not the rule.

There is a popular theory that the human race is being punished for the original sin committed by Adam in the garden of Eden. Judaism refutes that theory, claiming that God in His mercy would not curse the entire human race because of the sin of one primitive, untutored individual.

The word "Mitzvah" has assumed manifold meanings. Every conscientious Jew is eager to perform a "Mitzvah," or "a good turn," whenever there is an opportunity. A "Mitzvah" may be either a religious act, or an ethical gesture, or a charitable deed.

The term "Sin," though not much used in our daily conversation, plays an important part in religion. The Scriptures warn us repeatedly that the sinner is destined for punishment. Christian theologians tell us that the Day of Atonement is the Jewish solution to the problem of sin. Judaism is not completely in accord with that theory, but it maintains that Yom Kippur testifies to God's readiness to pardon sin, and to man's ability to abandon sin and re-create himself.

FOURTH PRINCIPLE

BELIEF IN THE IMMORTALITY OF THE SOUL

(This chapter is divided into four parts)

1. WE BELIEVE THAT MAN WAS CREATED IN THE IMAGE OF GOD

Man, the crown of creation, is endowed with a divine soul. We, as Jews, do not believe in the doctrine of the fall of man, nor in the need for a saviour; we maintain that the soul in man, emanating from God, lends sanctity to human existence. We also reject the theory that man must be redeemed because of the sins of the past. On the contrary, we stress the virtues of the past and the term "Z'chus Ovos," the "Virtues of the Fathers," has always played a prominent part in Jewish life.

2. WE BELIEVE THAT WHEN MAN DIES ONLY THE BODY DECAYS BUT THE SOUL, THE DIVINE IN MAN, IS ETERNAL AS GOD IS ETERNAL

Man is composed of two elements—body and soul. The body is perishable and mortal, but the soul is immortal because it is a part of the eternal light that never fails. "'Dust thou art, unto dust returnest,' was not spoken of the soul" (Longfellow). Many religious groups, Judaism included, lay stress upon the survival of the soul and intuitively accept the theory of immortality. Faith in the future destiny of the human soul is an important factor in religion, for while immortality is not an established fact, it is nevertheless a reasonable hope.

3. WE BELIEVE IN IMMORTALITY, THOUGH WE CANNOT DESCRIBE THE FORM IN WHICH THE SOUL CONTINUES ITS EXISTENCE

The eternal questions concerning immortality have occupied the human mind more than all the other mysteries which baffle the universe. Whenever we think about the continuance of life after death and about the destinies of the spirit in the hereafter we stand, dubious and perplexed, in the presence of a great mystery. Judaism has no set dogmas about life after death. Jewish theories about immortality vary from the speculative possibility of a spiritual life after death to a certainty of resurrection, or personal survival. Some Jewish thinkers are of the opinion that immortality is attained through the continued existence of a disembodied soul after death, while the staunch believers in the "resurrection" theory go to the extent of believing in the continuance of a physical existence in the realms of eternity.

"If a man dies, shall he live again?" Our answer is in the affirmative. We shall always believe in immortality, but we shall never be able to describe, with a degree of definiteness, the nature of the existence of the soul after it leaves its earthly frame.

4. WE BELIEVE THAT THE HUMAN SOUL IS DESTINED TO GIVE AN ACCOUNT OF ITSELF IN THE "OLOM HABBO"— THE FUTURE WORLD

We bury our dead with honors and express the hope that they may find divine recompense for noble deeds practiced on earth. The belief in reward and punishment is often linked with the belief in immortality, for the rabbis of the Talmud frequently stated that the real reward and the real punishment would be in the world to come, in the life after death. "Prepare thyself to meet thy Maker" was a slogan of the Jewish people throughout the ages, and many a Jew felt the importance of the quotation from the Ethics of the Fathers, "This world is but a hall-way, or an ante-room, before the big palace; prepare thyself in the ante-room so that thou mayest appear properly in the great palace" (Pirke Aboth 4:21).

NOTES ON RESURRECTION AND IMMORTALITY

(For Advanced Students and Adult Study Groups)

Religion has always concerned itself with man's destiny in the hereafter, but biblical Judaism merely admonishes the living to attain a state of holiness and does not speculate as to the future of the dead. The Old Testament, our Bible, does not speak of life after death.

The only statement in the Bible predicting a "resurrection" occurs in the book of Daniel, "And many of them that sleep in the dust of the earth shall awake, some to everlasting life, and some to reproaches and everlasting abhorrence" (12:2). In one of the books of the Apocrypha, "The Wisdom of Solomon," we have a direct statement on the theory of immortality, "Because God created man for incorruption, and made him an image of His own everlastingness, the souls of the righteous are in the hands of God. In the eyes of the foolish they seem to have died; but their hope is full of immortality." It is fair to assume, however, that Daniel and the author of "Wisdom" were greatly influenced by non-Jewish philosophies.

The theory of immortality came into Judaism through

contact with Greek thought. According to the Greek philosopher Plato, the soul exists before it enters the body. It is temporarily imprisoned within the body but liberated through death. It then returns to God to enjoy rewards for righteousness practiced on earth. Aristotle promises spiritual survival only to thinkers and great scholars. The Jewish Essenes, whose ascetic life was a combination of Greek philosophy and Jewish piety, maintained, according to the Talmud, that immortality was given only to those who offered their lives upon the altar of martyrdom.

While the Bible does not describe, nor promise, life after death, it contains many sayings which are indicative of a belief in survival. "The spirit returns unto God Who gave it" (Eccl. 12:7); "In the way of righteousness is life, and in the pathway thereof there is no death" (Proverbs 12:28); "He will swallow up death forever" (Isaiah 25:8). The psalmists frequently ask for immortality; Job expresses a wish for eternal life.

It was in the days of the Talmud that the theory of immortality was accepted in Israel. The Talmud speaks of immortality as "Ha-sharath Ha-nefesh" (survival of the soul), or "Chaye Olom" (eternal life). In Talmudic days the assurances of reward and punishment in the "Olom Habbo" became definitely fixed in the minds of the people. Speculation was then rampant as to what types of reward or punishment awaited the soul in the mysterious hereafter. "There is no rest for the righteous either in this life or in the next, but they go from strength to strength until they appear before God in Zion" (Berachoth 64).

Gan Eden, the Garden of Eden, the heavenly abode which God provided for Adam and Eve for their suste-

nance and happiness, became the Jewish symbol of
"Heaven" for the reward of saintly souls. Jewish literature is replete with descriptions of this imaginary place of
glory which awaits all saintly souls after their departure
from this earth.

Ge-henom or *Ge-henna* became the traditionally accepted symbol of "Hell" for the punishment of recal-
citrant Jewish souls. The Valley of Hinom or Henom
(Ge-henom), located in Jerusalem, was the place where
wicked kings like Menasseh (Kings II, 23:10) erected
fiery furnaces and caused children to be sacrificed in order to appease the wrath of Moloch, the god of fire. It was
also the place where the refuse of the city was burned.
That place where the fire burned incessantly and the
stench was unbearable, was so indescribably horrible that
our ancestors predicted a similar place for polluted, sin-
ful souls in the hereafter.

Chibut Hakever. There is also a Jewish theory that
there is a place in the hereafter which is neither Gan
Eden nor Ge-henom. This state of suspense, or of preparation of the soul, is known in Catholic eschatology as
purgatory, while in Judaism it is called "Chibut Hakever."

The word "Heaven" is translated in Hebrew "Shomayim" and is plural in character; hence the theory that
there are many heavens in the world above. The Talmud
states that martyrs will enjoy the glories of the seventh
heaven.

The theories of "Gilgul" or "Dibbuk," the belief in
the transmigration of a human soul into another human
body or, at times, into an animal, were reiterated in the
Cabbalah and were popularly accepted in many Jewish
circles in the last four centuries.

Traditional Judaism predicts that the resurrection of the dead will occur simultaneously with the coming of the Messiah. On that day, some Jews believe, all saintly Jewish souls, from all parts of the world, will be brought to Palestine to join the Messiah. Others maintain that only those pious men who were buried in the Holy Land will be revived. This latter theory is the source for the desire of pious Jews to be buried in Palestine.

Orthodox Jews have accepted the theory that "men will rise again, with their bodies fully revived." This theory, traditionally accepted in Israel through the ages and included in the creeds of Maimonides, is commonly referred to as personal "resurrection." The other theory, that of spiritual survival, is expressed by the word "immortality."

The medieval Jewish belief was in resurrection, rather than in immortality. The same view was held by Saadia Gaon (Emunoth V'deoth) and Judah Halevy (Kuzari). Moses Mendelssohn, the father of modern Judaism, expressed his belief in immortality, not in resurrection. Mendelssohn's views have been universally accepted by the followers of Reform Judaism, and the Union Prayer Book has eliminated from the "Amidah" every reference to resurrection.

The promise of immortality was not restricted to the Jewish people. The Talmud says that "the righteous men of the heathen nations will also have a share in the world to come."

We can neither prove, nor deny, the principle of immortality. However, it is traditionally accepted in Judaism that the soul of man which, in the biblical phrase, is "like the light of God," was not destined to be put out altogether. The words of Moses, "The Rock, His work is perfect," are recited at the Jewish funeral Service, indicating our faith in Him into Whose hands we commit the soul of man. The "Kaddish" and the "Yahrzeit," two established institutions in Israel, bear testimony to the Jewish belief in immortality.

FIFTH PRINCIPLE

(The belief in "Messiah" is divided into four parts)

1. WE BELIEVE THAT THE MESSIAH IDEA ALWAYS WAS, AND STILL IS, A DOMINANT FACTOR IN JEWISH LIFE

The Jewish people emerged as a group, or as a nation, with their deliverance from Egypt. The historic Exodus was a miraculous "Redemption," accomplished through the personality of Moses, the great "Redeemer."

In the year 586 B. C. the Kingdom of Judah was destroyed and the Jewish people were driven into the Babylonian exile. As they sat by the rivers of Babylon, they vowed eternal allegiance to Jerusalem. The Messiah idea became fixed in their minds, for they felt that the God of Israel Who freed their ancestors from Egypt would also redeem them from the Babylonian exile. And so it came to pass. They returned to Palestine, built the second Temple, and re-established the Jewish nation under the sovereignty of Cyrus who was subsequently referred to as the "Messiah" (Isaiah 45:1).

In the year 70 C. E. the Romans destroyed the second Temple and conquered the land of Judea. Our people then went into exile with the hope that God would again restore them to freedom and bring them back to the promised land as He had brought their ancestors to Palestine on two previous occasions.

In the course of time the Messianic idea became more

than a mere hope. It became, and remains to this day, an integral part of Jewish life and a vital factor in dominating Jewish thought and destiny.

2. We Believe That the Messiah Is yet To Come

In this creed we clash with that doctrine of Christianity which claims that the Messiah had already come. A Jewish man was once asked, "Why are you a Jew?" To which he promptly replied, "Because I am not a Christian." There is deep significance to this reply, for the loyal Jew clings to the creed of Maimonides, "I believe, with perfect faith, in the coming of the Messiah, and even though he tarries, I wait every day for his coming."

In recent years there has arisen a disagreement in Jewish circles as to whether there will be a Messiah or a Messianic Era. Orthodox Jews still believe in the eventual coming of a personal Messiah, or a *Goel*—a "Redeemer." Reform Jews do not believe in a personal Messiah, but they pray for a *Geulah*—a "Redemption." But whether we believe in a personal *Goel* or in a series of events that will bring about a *Geulah,* one thing is certain, and that is that the Jewish people persist in their hope for the coming of an ideal age when Israel, and all humanity, will enjoy the blessings of justice and peace.

3. We Believe That with the Coming of the Messianic Era Palestine Will Again Be Established as the National Jewish Homeland

For nearly nineteen centuries our people hoped and prayed for the return of the land of Israel to the children of Israel. They persisted in their belief that with the coming of the Messiah would also come the restoration of the land of Palestine to the Jewish people. However, when the Zionist organization, under the leadership of Dr. Theodor Herzl, announced its adoption of the Basle program (the establishment of a national Jewish home in Palestine), there was considerable opposition from many Jewish groups. The orthodox group resented the "secularism" of the Zionist movement and the reform leaders took exception to its "nationalism." These oppositions, though still prevalent, have been greatly minimized in recent years due to the unfortunate developments in Jewish life. Now it is generally conceded that the Messianic hope, preserved through the ages, is approaching its realization, facilitated by the Zionist movement which is making considerable progress toward the establishment of a national Jewish homeland in Palestine.

4. WE BELIEVE THAT THE MESSIANIC ERA WILL BRING PEACE AND HAPPINESS NOT ONLY TO ISRAEL BUT TO THE ENTIRE HUMAN RACE

The prophets who presaged the benefits of the Messianic Era promised little to the individual, but stressed the future welfare of the nation and of all mankind. Isaiah predicted that the time will come when "people will beat their swords into plowshares, and their spears into pruninghooks, nation shall not lift up sword against nation, neither shall they learn war any more" (Isaiah 2:4). He further visualized the day when "the wolf shall dwell with the lamb . . ." (Isaiah 11:9).

The Messianic hope promises freedom and happiness to Israel in "a world of peace." The position of the Jew in the world may change with the times, but his Messianic creed will remain substantially the same. As long as injustice prevails in human relationships, as long as people are dominated by malice and hatred, as long as wars are waged among nations, as long as people resort to brutality and bloodshed in settling disputes, so long will Israel assert that the Jewish people, and all humanity, are in need of a Messiah and that the Messianic Era is yet to come.

NOTES ON THE MESSIANIC CREED

(For Advanced Students and Adult Study Groups)

The survival of the Jew is largely due to the Messiah idea. It gave him something to hope for; it bolstered up his spirit and gave him courage to endure the indignities that were heaped upon him by an unfriendly world.

The relentless claim of the Jewish people to Palestine was always assailed by the church. The insulting word, "HEP," an acrostic composed of the initial letters of *H*ierosolyma *E*st *P*erdita (Jerusalem is lost) was used by the Crusaders when they attacked the Jews.

There is an allegorical saying in the Talmud, "Messiah was born on the day when the Temple at Jerusalem was destroyed" (Yerush. Ber. 2), indicating that the birth of Israel's eternal hope occurred on the day of Israel's greatest calamity.

The nineteenth century, the period of Jewish emancipation, witnessed the development of four new movements in Israel, each giving its interpretation of the Messianic idea: (1) The Assimilationist Movement, in its efforts to prepare the Jewish people for citizenship and for political equality in the Western countries of Europe, declared that the Messianic idea is antiquated and obsolete. (2) The Reform Movement adopted a policy in which the Jewish people were declared to be a religious group, not a nation. The prayers were changed so as to eliminate every mention of Zion or Jerusalem, the personal Messiah idea was abandoned, but the hope for the coming of a Messianic Era was retained. (3) The Haskalah Movement, aiming to introduce secular culture and "enlightenment" among the Jews of Russia and Poland, ridiculed the prayers and ceremonies of "religious" Messianism, but paved the way for a "national" Messianism, for a secular love of Zion. (4) The Zionist Movement evolved a modern interpretation of the Messianic creed. It took an old hope and diverted it into new channels. It minimized the importance of "prayer" for Zion and emphasized the need of "action" for Zion. It called for the return of Palestine to the Jewish people who, through the Messianic hope, have never relinquished their claim to Palestine.

Jewish tradition promises the "resurrection" of the righteous with the coming of the Messiah. Chassidim and mystics speak of the great "Feast" that will be held on the day when the Messiah will come. They even describe the kind of food and the type of wine that will be served at that "Feast."

There were many false Messiahs in the history of our people; the best known of them are Bar Kochba and Sabbatai Zevi.

The Messiah idea is annually revived with the observance of Rosh Hashanah. On that day we pray, "O God, blow a great shofar for our redemption." This was taken to indicate that a loud shofar will be blown on the day of the coming of the Messiah (Shofar shel Moshiach).

PART TWO

LAWS AND OBSERVANCES OF JUDAISM

LAWS AND OBSERVANCES OF JUDAISM

INTRODUCTION

Judaism has a series of laws which regulate the religious observances of the people of Israel. Principles of faith are theories in which we believe, but observances are religious acts which we practice.

There are rites and ceremonies in every religion, but in Judaism they occupy a place of unusual importance and are usually considered religious "laws." The biblical commandments, "Thou shalt keep" and "Thou shalt observe" constitute a complete code of Jewish legalism, a code which has been adhered to by the Jewish people through all their history. In Judaism every ceremonial or religious law, ordered in the Bible and substantiated in the Talmud, is considered of divine origin, ordained by God for the spiritual and moral guidance of the Jewish people. Every Jewish observance, whatever its nature, is a means through which the Jew manifests his loyalty to his religion.

The laws and observances of Judaism regulate the life of the Jew from the cradle to the grave. If, through the ages, the Jew has been different from his Gentile neighbor, it has been because of the distinctive qualities of the ceremonies of the Jewish faith. The observant Jew does not only profess his religion—he lives it; his entire life is circumscribed by a series of observances.

The ceremonial duties of Judaism are performed in many ways. They are solemnized in the synagogue and in

57

the home through public and private worship; they are
carried out by means of the traditional observance of the
Sabbath and of the holidays; they are observed through
the customs and symbols of Jewish life; they are especially
performed through the dietary laws which regulate the
physical life of each individual Jew. We have, therefore,
divided the material on the "Laws and Observances of
Judaism" into the following chapters: (1) The Importance of Prayer, (2) The Synagogue, (3) The Jewish
Home, (4) The Sabbath, (5) The Jewish Calendar, (6)
Rosh Hashanah, (7) Yom Kippur, (8) Passover, (9) Shavuos, (10) Succos, (11) Chanukah, (12) Purim, (13) Special Days, (14) The Dietary Laws.

1. THE IMPORTANCE OF PRAYER

Prayer is the ceremonial expression of religion, the link which unites man with his Creator. It is in prayer that man expresses his yearning for God in times of need and his gratitude to God in times of joy. Every prayer is offered on the presumption that it will be heard by God on high, although we are unable to determine the extent to which the decrees of God may be influenced or changed by it. Prayer is not always a simple act of asking. It is a combination of human emotions by means of which man expresses his attitude towards God and is comprised of such things as praise, reverence, humility, gratitude, and petition. The admonition to serve the Lord "with all thy heart" means to serve Him through prayer, the expression of the heart.

Judaism maintains that the utterance of a prayer is a meritorious act in itself because it ennobles the human soul and endows it with faith in God. Of course, we must realize that there is a continuous clash in human desires and that quite frequently individuals or nations simultaneously pray for mutually contradictory things. Under such circumstances it is natural that the fulfillment of a certain petition may please one person or group, but cause consternation among the people who prayed for its opposite. It therefore becomes the duty of man to develop a spirit of faith and to yield to the wisdom of the universal Ruler Who grants one petition and rejects another. No doubt of the efficacy of prayer can arise in the devout spirit.

The Jewish ceremonies of worship differ from the ceremonies of other religions because the ritual of Judaism is distinctive. Our people pray in many languages, but Hebrew is our classic language of prayer and our liturgy, as contained in the Siddur and in the Machzor, is a colorful one. While it is permissible to offer prayer in the solitude of the home, we prefer to do so in the synagogue, in the presence of a congregation (Minyan).

The liturgical forms of our organized Services, though regulated by tradition, have been subjected to many changes and variations. In the old world there were three types of Jews—Ashkenazim, Sephardim, Chassidim—all of them following different rituals; in America there are also three groups of Jews—Orthodox, Conservative, Reform—with equal variety in their forms of worship. The frequency of synagogue attendance for worship also differs greatly in Jewish life. Our orthodox brethren worship three times daily—Shacharis, Mincha, Maariv—while progressive Jews find it sufficient to pray only on the Sabbath, or even limit their synagogue attendance to the High Holidays. But whether we pray daily or at certain intervals, we are required to recognize the fact that the act of worship is a religious ceremony obligatory upon every Jew. "God is nigh unto them that call upon Him, to all that call upon Him in truth" (Ps. 145:18).

2. THE SYNAGOGUE

The Jewish people are interested in many endeavors
—religious, charitable, and communal—but the synagogue is the true center of all Jewish activities. The
historic changes within Judaism and the variety of cultures and standards among different types of Jews have
brought about many variations in the observance of
Jewish ceremonies, but the position of the synagogue
as the center of Jewish life has remained unchanged.
From the days of the Babylonian exile down to the
present day, the synagogue, humble and unassuming
though it often may be, has brought divine inspiration
and spiritual comfort to the children of Israel in all the
lands of their dispersion. The synagogue functions as
a House of Worship, as a House of Assembly, as a House
of Study.

HOUSE OF WORSHIP

The synagogue is, first and foremost, a House of Worship (Beth T'fillah). Prayer is the noblest expression of
the human soul. Man, realizing his limitations in the
vastness of the universe, is naturally inclined to worship
a power greater than his own. Judaism has compiled a
voluminous liturgy of assorted prayers, and it has also
emphasized the importance of public worship, proclaim-
ing it the fundamental expression of ceremonial religion. And while Judaism permits the Jew to recite his
daily prayers in the privacy of his home, or even under
the open sky, it recommends that every Jew go to the

synagogue where ten men are present to make up the "Minyan" necessary for public worship. When such a "public" service is held, the "K'dusha" is heard when the "Amidah" is repeated; the Torah is read; the Kaddish is recited; public functions such as weddings and Barmitzvahs are held. In this connection it may be stated that one of the reasons why the Jewish people have always preferred to live in cities rather than in rural districts is the desire of the observant Jew for the companionship of his people and the benefits of the synagogue.

In the synagogue all Jews are alike before God. Ten male Jews above the age of thirteen, whether they be learned men or illiterates, saints or sinners, constitute the necessary quorum (Minyan) for public worship. The leader of the Service need not be a rabbi or a cantor. Any Jew who knows the ritual is eligible to lead in public worship. To offset a frequent accusation of our adversaries about the alleged "unity" in universal Judaism, it should be stated that there is neither a synod nor a hierarchy in Israel. No rabbi or functionary of the synagogue is required to take orders from a superior dignitary. Only in Great Britain is there a "chief" rabbi. However, his title and his position are determined by the British government, not by the Jewish people. Each synagogue in Israel is controlled by a congregation that is independent and autonomous, and each synagogue may reach its own decisions on all matters of procedure, including the ritual.

Because of strict adherence to the second commandment, "Thou shalt not make unto thyself any graven image nor any likeness , , , ," Judaism has banished from the synagogue all paintings or statues which might lead the people to idol worship. Nevertheless, the synagogue contains a number of symbols and sacred articles which are either displayed or used in connection with the performance of the ceremonies of Judaism. (See "Symbols.")

HOUSE OF ASSEMBLY

In Hebrew the synagogue is popularly known as the "Beth Haknesses" (House of Assembly). The synagogue has always been, and still is, a meeting place for gatherings of all kinds. Our people may make use of public halls on certain occasions, but the synagogue is the natural place of assembly for religious, semi-religious, or social celebrations. It is also used as a meeting place for the discussion of matters pertaining to the community welfare. It may be a coincidence that the early Puritans in North America, influenced by Mosaic legislation, called their churches Meeting Houses.

HOUSE OF STUDY

Another important function of the synagogue is to provide facilities for our people to study the Torah. As a House of Study (Beth Hamidrash) the synagogue is the home of the Jewish soul. Judaism is not merely a religion of rites and ceremonies; it is primarily a religion of culture and of spiritual enlightenment. In fact, there are many scholarly Jews in Europe, especially in Lithuania, who minimize the importance of prayer and prefer to spend their time in the study of the Talmud. The synagogue, as a house of study, usually has a large collection of books, such as the Pentateuch, the Commentaries, the Midrash, the Talmud, etc., and these books are used over and over again by the people who come to the House of God.

The Jews are possibly the only people in the world who consider the act of reading or studying the books of sacred literature as a religious act, or "Mitzvah," in itself. To other people the reading of a sacred book is very much like the studying of any other subject, a process which leads to mental development, to self improvement, or to sheer pleasure. In Judaism the study of the Torah is repeatedly urged not only because "learning" is a religious act in itself, but also because the knowledge of our ceremonies leads to their observance. The Jewish people are frequently called, and rightfully so, the "people" of the Book, and the synagogue may properly be designated as the "home" of the Book.

3. THE JEWISH HOME

Judaism is not merely a religion. It is a constitution which regulates the entire mode of life of the Jewish people. The home, the center of physical life, is, with the synagogue, the center of Jewish ceremonial life. The Jew does not assume that he finds God when he enters the synagogue and abandons Him when he leaves. His religion is continuous and reminds him daily that, "Thou shalt speak of them (the words of God) when thou sittest in thy house, when thou walkest by the way, when thou liest down, and when thou risest up" (Deut. 6:7). Like the synagogue, the Jewish home is frequently referred to as a "Temple in miniature," for the religious and ceremonial laws of Judaism are actually observed there. History has convinced us that Jewish traditional ceremonies are perpetuated not only in the synagogue or in the religious school, but in the Jewish home as well.

THE SABBATH

Most of the laws and regulations pertaining to the observance of the Sabbath are carried out in the Jewish home. (See Section 4.) When the home is prepared and the table is properly set for the Sabbath, a spirit of rest and holiness prevails. Special food, prepared for the Sabbath, is an essential element in the ceremonial observance of the sacred day.

THE HOLIDAYS

The home also plays a prominent part in the observance of the Jewish holidays. The solemnity of the High

Holidays is felt not only in the synagogue, but also in the home. For the Passover festival there are many preparations in the home, and the Seder, the most elaborate Jewish observance of the year, is definitely a home ceremony. Even the Succah, the substitute for the home during the week of Succos, actually symbolizes the temporary home of our ancestors in the wilderness. On Chanukah, the Jewish home is usually the scene of family reunions, with games and entertainments contributing to the joyous spirit of the holiday. Purim is a happy festival characterized by bounteous spreads of food and drink. In fact, the ceremonial observances of every Jewish holiday is complete only when the home cooperates with the synagogue.

The Dietary Laws

The home plays its most conspicuous part in ceremonial Judaism in the observance of the Jewish dietary laws. (See Section 14.) It has often been stated that the attitude of the Jew towards the dietary laws is a barometer indicating his loyalty to the faith of his fathers. Those of our people who assail this part of our faith and refer to it as "kitchen Judaism" fail to realize that the observance of the dietary laws has made the Jewish home a place where the influence of religion is constantly felt. In fact, today when our people do not go to the synagogue frequently, nor recite their prayers regularly, there is a positive practice of Jewish ceremonies only in those homes where the dietary laws are observed.

The Jewish home is the place where prayers are recited, either regularly or on certain occasions; where "Grace" is offered before and after meals; where intemperance and drunkenness are conspicuously absent; where the members of the family are loyal and devoted to each other. (See "Symbols and Practices in the Jewish Home.")

4. THE SABBATH

Origin of the Sabbath

**THE OBSERVANCE OF THE SABBATH WAS THE FIRST RE-
LIGIOUS ORDER GIVEN BY GOD UNTO ISRAEL**

According to the biblical theory of Genesis, God created the world in six days and rested on the seventh day.
He then blessed the Sabbath day and hallowed it as a
day of rest for all generations to come (Gen. 2:1–4).
History tells us that our ancestors were ordered to keep
the Sabbath even before they were given the ten commandments on Mt. Sinai, for they were told to refrain
from gathering or cooking the Manna on the seventh
day (Ex. 16:22–31). The fourth commandment subsequently admonished the people of Israel to "remember
the Sabbath day and keep it holy" (Ex. 20:8).

Importance of the Sabbath

**BY THE OBSERVANCE OF THE SABBATH WE MANIFEST OUR
BELIEF IN GOD AS THE CREATOR OF THE WORLD**

The Bible tells us that the Sabbath is a "symbol" between God and Israel, that "in six days the Lord made
heaven and earth, and on the seventh day He ceased from
work and rested" (Ex. 31:17). The rabbis even go to the
extent of saying that he who disregards the Sabbath and
desecrates it is considered to have denied the existence
of God.

FRIDAY EVENING

THE SABBATH COMMENCES ON FRIDAY EVENING, AT SUN-
SET, AND TERMINATES SATURDAY AT SUNSET

In the Jewish calendar the days are counted so that the night belongs to the succeeding day. By doing so, we follow the process recorded in the order of creation, where it says, "and it was evening, and it was morning, one day" (Gen. 1:5).

SABBATH CANDLES

THE SABBATH IS USHERED IN WITH SPECIAL LIGHTS OVER WHICH THE HOUSEWIFE PRONOUNCES A BLESSING

Reasons for Lighting the Sabbath Candles

(1) As no fire is to be kindled on the Sabbath, the candles are lit before the Sabbath sets in.
(2) Light is conducive to that spiritual joy which prevails in every Jewish home on the Sabbath.
(3) Light is the symbol of the Torah and of religious enlightenment (Prov. 6:23).

Why the Sabbath Candles Are Lit by the Housewife

(1) The woman makes the home and establishes its pleasant associations. She was therefore accorded the privilege of illuminating the home for the Sabbath joy.
(2) The woman (Eve) has dimmed the light of the world by tempting man to sin; she is to redeem herself by kindling the sacred Sabbath lights.

Ceremony of Lighting the Candles

(1) When lighting the Sabbath candles, the woman utters a benediction which is her acceptance of the Sab-

bath and which restrains her from kindling a fire. Therefore, she lights the candles first and then pronounces the
"Brochoh."

(2) It is an accepted rule that the Jew must not enjoy
anything unless he first thanks God for it. The Jewish
woman therefore closes her eyes and does not see the
light until after she recites the blessing and the prayer
accompanying it.

(3) Tradition calls for the lighting of two Sabbath candles, yet there are many countries where the Jewish
woman lights one candle for each member of her household.

(4) The ceremony of lighting the candles, originally instituted for the Sabbath, has subsequently been extended
to include the festivals and the High Holidays.

DAY OF REST

THE SABBATH IS A DAY OF REST AND OF PHYSICAL RECRE-
ATION

We were commanded by God to work six days and to
rest on the seventh day. Not only we but also those in our
employ and the animals that work for us must abstain
from every form of labor on the Sabbath day.

There were thirty-nine different kinds of labor involved in the process of building the Tabernacle. The
rabbis of the Talmud therefore ordained that any work
that is the same as or similar to any of those thirty-nine
types of labor shall not be performed on the Sabbath
day.

The Sabbath laws of rest may be set aside (a) in case of
severe illness, (b) in case of a fire or any other emergency

that threatens imminent danger, (c) in the prosecution of a just war.

DAY OF JOY

THE SABBATH IS A DAY OF JOY AND HAPPINESS

Oneg Shabbat, "the delight of the Sabbath," is a popular expression which gives the true meaning of the day. Despite the vicissitudes which the Jew was forced to endure because of his loyalty to the Sabbath, and despite the restrictions and inconveniences which the observance of the Sabbath entails, the Jew always experiences a weekly rejuvenation in "the delight of the Sabbath."

In the synagogue, the Sabbath is ushered in with the "L'cho Dodi," a prayer in which the bride (Sabbath) is joyously welcomed by the groom (Israel). In the home, the Sabbath is happily received at the Friday evening meal with the traditional cup of wine and with the recitation of the Kiddush, a prayer in which the sanctity of the Sabbath is announced and thanks are offered to God for the holy day which brings bodily repose and spiritual delight to Israel. Festive garments, a clean home, good food, and the family reunion at the festive board create a happy atmosphere in the Jewish home "in honor of the Sabbath." Fasting, for whatever cause, is forbidden except on the Day of Atonement; the sitting of Shivah, or any other manifestation of mourning, is likewise forbidden. It is also customary to share the joy of the day with an "Orach," a Sabbath guest. The Talmud goes to the extent of saying that the joy of the Sabbath is a foretaste of the divine happiness in the world to come.

Day of Holiness

THE SABBATH IS A DAY OF HOLINESS AND OF SPIRITUAL RECREATION

The Sabbath is not only a day of rest and of joy, but also a day of consecration. It is devoted, by the observant Jew, to the study of the Bible, of the Talmud, and of other sources of Jewish lore. The Sedrah, the weekly portion of the Torah, is usually read and its commentaries studied; sermons and religious discourses are an important part of the program of the holy day.

Every Jew is required to attend divine Services on Friday evening, Saturday morning, and Saturday afternoon. The Friday evening Service consists of "Kabolas Shabbos"—welcoming the Sabbath—and the "Maariv"— evening prayer. The Sabbath morning Service comprises the "Shacharis" (morning prayer), the reading of the Sedrah from the Torah, the reading of a chapter from the Prophets (Haphtorah), and the "Mussaf" (additional prayer). The "Mincha" or afternoon prayer consists of the "Ashrei," the reading of a small portion of the Torah, the "Amidah," and the "Aleinu."

The Torah has been divided, since the days of the second Temple, into fifty-four portions, or Sedrahs. On each Sabbath one portion (occasionally two) is read, and eight men are called up to pronounce the benediction over the Torah. The eighth one is called "Maftir" because he recites the Haphtorah; this honor is usually conferred upon a boy when he reaches the age of thirteen (Bar Mitzvah).

HAVDALAH

AT THE CONCLUSION OF THE SABBATH, THE HAVDALAH
PRAYER IS RECITED OVER A CUP OF WINE

Havdalah means "distinction." In this prayer we offer
thanks to God for the distinction He made between the
Sabbath and the week days. Since our six-day period of
creative work commences on Saturday night, the Havdalah also contains a prayer of gratitude for light, God's
first accomplishment in the creation of the world. As a
part of the Havdalah ceremony, we approach the light
and look at our finger nails, so that the "Brochoh" over
light shall not have been pronounced in vain. We also
smell incense or spices in order to revive the soul which
is depressed at the departure of the Sabbath.

NOTES ON THE SABBATH

(For Advanced Students and Adult Study Groups)

In biblical days, the Sabbath laws were rigidly adhered to. Death or excommunication was the penalty
for profaning the Sabbath by work (see Num. 15:32).

It has frequently been stated that while the Jewish
people observed and perpetuated the Sabbath, it was, in
turn, the Sabbath which preserved the Jewish people.

The Psalmist tells us that wine "gladdens" the heart
of man, while bread "sustains" his heart (Ps. 104:15). It
has therefore been ruled by the rabbis that when wine
for the Kiddush is not available, the prayer may be recited over bread.

In commenting upon the Sabbath as a day of joy, the
rabbis went to the extent of stating that the Jew possesses

an "additional soul" (Neshomoh Yesseira) on the Sabbath day.

There are many groups of devout Christians who observe Saturday as a day of rest because they believe that the seventh day of the week, and not the first, is the original Sabbath of the Bible.

On Friday evening we sing the popular "Sholom Aleichem," bidding welcome to the good angels which, according to legend, accompany us from the synagogue to the home.

"Oneg Shabbat," literally "the delight of the Sabbath," is the name given to Sabbath parties held in the synagogue or in the home. The Oneg Shabbat party usually combines an intellectual program with a festive spirit.

(See "Customs and Symbols of the Sabbath.")

5. THE JEWISH CALENDAR

The Jewish calendar is composed of twelve months, with either twenty-nine or thirty days in each month. In the case of a leap year another month, the second Adar, is added. Each month is hereby given, together with its special days or observances.

Nissan   Festival of Passover—Fifteenth day to the twenty-third.

Iyar   Lag B'omer—Eighteenth day.

Sivan   Festival of Shavuos—Sixth and Seventh days.

Tammuz   Fast of Tammuz—Seventeenth day.

Ab   Tisha B'Ab, the black fast—The ninth day.

Ellul

Tishri   Rosh Hashanah—First and Second days.
Fast of G'daliah—Third day.
Yom Kippur—Tenth day.
Festival of Succos—Fifteenth day to the twenty-fourth.

Cheshvan

Kislev   Chanukah—Begins on the twenty-fifth day.

Tebeth   Fast of Tebeth—Tenth day.

Shevat	Chamishoh Ossor B'Shevat (Jewish Arbor Day)—Fifteenth day.
Adar	Fast of Esther—Thirteenth day. Purim—Fourteenth day.

Adar II	In a leap year.

---

6. ROSH HASHANAH

DATE AND NAME

ROSH HASHANAH, THE JEWISH NEW YEAR'S CELEBRATION, OCCURS ON THE FIRST TWO DAYS OF TISHRI

"Rosh" means head or beginning; "Hashanah," of the year. Rosh Hashanah therefore signifies the day which marks the beginning of the New Year.

While Nissan is the first month of the biblical, civil year, Tishri is the first month of the traditional, religious year.

TWO DAYS

ROSH HASHANAH IS UNIVERSALLY OBSERVED FOR TWO DAYS

As our ancestors were uncertain which was the first day of the month, they ordered that Rosh Hashanah be observed for two days. The rabbis of the Talmud subsequently declared that the two days of Rosh Hashanah are to be considered as "one long day."

BIBLICAL AND TRADITIONAL

THE OBSERVANCE OF ROSH HASHANAH, IN ITS PRESENT FORM, IS NOT SO MUCH BIBLICAL AS IT IS TRADITIONAL

The Bible speaks of the first day of the seventh month as "a day of blowing the trumpet" (Numb. 29:1) or as "a memorial of the blowing of the trumpet" (Levit. 23:24). Tradition, however, has established the following reasons for the observance of Rosh Hashanah:

(a) The Creation of the World commenced on the

first day of Tishri according to the traditional version.

(b) It is the seventh Rosh Chodesh, or New Moon. And just as the seventh day of the week is holy (Sabbath), and just as the seventh year is of special significance (Shmitah), so was extraordinary sanctity attached to the seventh Rosh Chodesh of the year.

(c) The celebration of the arrival of the fiftieth year, known as the Jubilee Year, was held in the month of Tishri; slaves were liberated, and all land which had been sold within the fifty years reverted to the original owners or their heirs.

SOLEMNITY AND HOLINESS

ROSH HASHANAH IS A DAY OF SOLEMNITY AND HOLINESS

On Rosh Hashanah the Jew gives himself to serious thought, to meditation, to prayer. He makes an inventory of his spiritual life; he reflects upon his deeds during the past year; and he resolves to improve his ways in the year to come. In describing the importance of the day, Rosh Hashanah is known by three names: (a) Day of Judgment, (b) Day of Memorial, (c) Day of Blowing the Shofar.

DAY OF JUDGMENT

ROSH HASHANAH IS TRADITIONALLY KNOWN AS THE DAY OF JUDGMENT. (YOM HADDIN)

The symbol of the month of Tishri is a pair of scales. There is a Jewish tradition that on Rosh Hashanah God weighs and measures the merits and faults of the Jew and then passes judgment upon him, determining his fate in the coming year.

Malchuyoth. The first part of the Mussaph Service, known as Malchuyoth, extols God as the sole Ruler and Supreme Judge of the universe, thus emphasizing the significance of Rosh Hashanah as the Day of Judgment.

DAY OF REMEMBRANCE

ROSH HASHANAH IS BEST KNOWN IN OUR LITURGY AS THE DAY OF REMEMBRANCE. (YOM HAZIKORON)

The biblical term, "a memorial of blowing the Shofar," indicates that on that day we are to remember the important experiences of our lives, draw valuable lessons from them, and utilize them for the service of God. We are also to "remember that we are but dust," that we are frail and insignificant in the hands of God.

Zichronoth. The second part of the Mussaph Service, Zichronoth, stresses the importance of Rosh Hashanah as a Day of Memorial. On that day the Jew remembers his past and plans for his future. He is, in turn, remembered by God. Tradition tells us that on Remembrance Day God perceives, notes, and remembers all His children and also provides for their needs. Every act of the past is recalled, every concealed mystery is revealed on that day when "the memorial of all His creatures comes before Him and He taketh cognizance of all their actions."

DAY OF BLOWING THE SHOFAR

IN THE BIBLE ROSH HASHANAH IS DESCRIBED AS THE "DAY OF BLOWING THE SHOFAR." (YOM T'RUOH.)

The Shofar is blown on Rosh Hashanah in accordance with a biblical command and constitutes the most prominent feature of the observance of the day. The following reasons have been given for the blowing of the Shofar:

(a) To awaken us from our lethargy and arouse us to an enthusiastic attitude toward spiritual values and religious observances. Maimonides declared that the Shofar sounds an alarm and says, "Awake, ye sleepers, and ponder your deeds; remember your Creator and come back to Him in penitence."

(b) To confuse Satan and to frustrate the accusations which he brings against us on the Day of Judgment.

(c) To remind us of the Revelation on Mt. Sinai when God gave unto Israel the Ten Commandments amidst the loud sounds of the Shofar. It is thus an exhortation to consecrate ourselves anew to the service of God and to the performance of His commandments.

(d) The Shofar, made of the ram's horn, recalls the biblical narrative in which Abraham was ready to sacrifice his son Isaac, but, in obedience to the will of God, offered a ram as a substitute. The stories of the birth of Isaac and of the "Akedah" (the intended sacrifice of Isaac) are read in the synagogue on the first and second days of Rosh Hashanah.

Shoferoth. The third part of the Mussaph Service, the Shoferoth, refers to Rosh Hashanah as the day of blowing the Shofar and describes historic occasions on which the clarion call of the Shofar was heard.

DIVINE SERVICES

IT IS THE DUTY OF EVERY JEW TO PARTICIPATE IN DIVINE SERVICES ON ROSH HASHANAH

In the morning, we go to the synagogue early. We pray "Shacharis" (first half of the Services), read a portion of the Torah, then the Haphtorah, blow the Shofar, and pray Mussaph (second half of the Service). A sermon is generally delivered prior to the Mussaph Service. In the afternoon, we pray Minchah.

L'SHONOH TOVOH TIKOSSEIVU

THE FORM OF FELICITATION ON ROSH HASHANAH IS "L'SHONOH TOVOH TIKOSSEIVU"

A universally accepted Jewish tradition has it that three books are open before God on Rosh Hashanah. The good people are inscribed in the book of life; the wicked people are doomed to death; those in the middle of the road are given an opportunity to repent during the ten days of penitence. Hence the wish "L'shonoh Tovoh Tikosseivu" which literally means, "may you be inscribed in the book for a happy year." Greetings are generally exchanged on this solemn, yet joyous occasion. Family affections are fostered, friendly relations are renewed, and the bonds of Jewish brotherhood are strengthened.

TASHLICH

IT IS AN ESTABLISHED CUSTOM IN ISRAEL TO "CAST THE SINS" INTO A RIVER ON ROSH HASHANAH

Some of our brethren assemble along the banks of a running water on the afternoon of Rosh Hashanah and recite biblical verses and appropriate penitential prayers. They also shake their garments as if casting their sins into the water. This custom, known as Tashlich, was established in accordance with the prophecy of Micah (Micah 17:19) "He will again have compassion on us; He will subdue our iniquities; and Thou wilt cast (Ve-Tashlich) all their sins in the depths of the sea."

TEN DAYS OF PENITENCE

THE TEN DAYS FROM ROSH HASHANAH THROUGH YOM KIP-
PUR ARE KNOWN AS THE DAYS OF PENITENCE

In those days we are to repent of our evil deeds and
resolve to do better in the future. The Sabbath between
Rosh Hashanah and Yom Kippur is called "Sabbath
Shuvah" because the Haphtorah of the day begins with
the words, "Shuvah Yisroel." It says, "Return, O Israel,
unto the Lord, thy God" (Hosea 14:2).

NOTES ON ROSH HASHANAH

(For Advanced Students and Adult Study Groups)

The month of Ellul, preceding Rosh Hashanah, is a
season of preparation for the Solemn Days. "Prepare thyself to meet thy God, O Israel," is the motto of the month
of Ellul. "L'dovid Ori," a psalm in which the Jew expresses his unshaken faith in God's salvation (Ps. 27), is
recited daily after evening and morning Services, and the
Shofar is blown in the synagogue every week-day after the
morning Service. It is also customary in Israel to visit the
cemetery and to recite prayers at the graves of parents
during the month of Ellul.

"Slichos," a series of penitential prayers, are recited
every day, early in the morning, for one week prior to
Rosh Hashanah.

The "Machzor," the collection of prayers comprising
the liturgy of Rosh Hashanah, contains many prayers
and poems that were composed in the tragic days of the
Middle Ages. The "Unsanne Tokeff," written by Rabbi

Amnon, a famous martyr, commemorates an important chapter in the history of Jewish martyrdom.

The biblical narratives of the birth of Isaac and of his intended sacrifice are read on the two days of Rosh Hashanah not only to remind us of the ram, but also because, according to tradition, both events occurred on the first day of Tishri. As the birth of Samuel is also supposed to have happened on that day, we read, as the Haphtorah of the first day, the first chapter of the Book of Samuel.

The Shofar is an instrument of sound and is not to be used on the Sabbath day. Therefore when Rosh Hashanah falls on Saturday, the blowing of the Shofar is omitted.

It is customary in Israel to eat sweet food on Rosh Hashanah. After the Maariv Service in the evening, the family gathers around the festive board. Kiddush is recited and honey, or sweet fruit, is eaten and the wish is expressed that "it may be the will of God to renew unto us a sweet, pleasant year."

Rosh Hashanah and Yom Kippur are known as the High Holidays. They are also known by the Hebrew name of Yomim Noroim—"Days of Awe" or "Solemn Days."

7. YOM KIPPUR

DATE

YOM KIPPUR, THE DAY OF ATONEMENT, FALLS ON THE
TENTH DAY OF TISHRI

Yom Kippur is the last day and the climax of the ten
days of penitence which are collectively known as the
Penitential Season.

HOLIEST DAY

YOM KIPPUR WAS ORDAINED BY GOD AS THE HOLIEST DAY
OF THE YEAR

The Talmud speaks of Yom Kippur as "Yoma"—"The
Day," or "The Great Day." In the Torah it is called
"Shabbos Shabboson," the Sabbath of Sabbaths. No work
of any kind is to be performed on Yom Kippur because
on that day we dedicate our entire being, body and soul,
to obtaining God's pardon for sins committed. "On this
day God will forgive you and cleanse you from all your
sins, that you may be clean before the Lord" (Lev. 16:30).

ESSENTIAL CHARACTERISTICS OF THE DAY:

CONFESSION OF SIN. (*Vidui.*)

On Yom Kippur the Jew examines himself and dis-
covers his failings. Then, conscious of his sins, he seeks
reconciliation with God. Humiliated and contrite of
spirit, he confesses his sins, not to a mortal like himself,
but to his Heavenly Father. The Confession of Sin is
repeated many times during the day and includes sins

committed against God and against our fellow men. But while we may obtain atonement for sins committed against God, we cannot wipe out the sins against our fellow men until we rectify the wrongs done.

Our confessions of sin are recited in the plural or collective form (Chotonu, Oshamnu— We have sinned, we have trespassed), indicating that each Jew bears the burden of responsibility for the transgression of all the Jewish people in all parts of the world.

REPENTANCE. (*T'shuvah*.)

Confession of sins means nothing unless we sincerely repent of our evil deeds and resolve not to commit them again. We have the assurance that God, our merciful Father, will always receive us in His favor when we return unto Him in repentance. "Return and live!" is the terse admonition of the prophet (Ez. 18:32). According to the Talmud, the "Baal T'shuvah," the repentant sinner who changes his mode of life and turns to be a religious man, stands higher in the esteem of God than the person who was always pious and law-abiding.

FASTING. (*Tzom*.)

God ordered us to "afflict our souls" from the evening of the ninth to the evening of the tenth day of Tishri. The biblical term, "afflict the soul," is synonymous with fasting, for we can most effectively afflict ourselves and approach nearer to God by depriving our bodies of necessary nourishment. When Moses interceded in behalf of the children of Israel, imploring God's atonement for their sins, he fasted forty days. The prophet Isaiah tells us, in the Haphtorah of Yom Kippur, that fasting should soften our hearts so that we may sympathize with the

needy and share our bread with the hungry (Isaiah 58).
On this Day of God when the body is denied all food and
drink, the divine within us, the soul, is brought into
closer contact with its Maker.

ATONEMENT—GOD'S PARDON. (*Kippur*.)

The Yom Kippur "Machzor" contains this significant
statement, "It is because of Thy great love for us, O God,
Thou hast given unto us this Day of Atonement, a day
in which our iniquities are forgiven and our sins are
pardoned." Judaism does not believe that the sinner is
condemned to eternal doom. He is given an opportunity
to repent and earn the blessing of divine remission. In
the times of the Talmud, Yom Kippur was celebrated as
a happy time of religious ecstasy, and to this very day the
thoughts of a new life, of a purified soul, and of a happy
reconciliation with God create a spirit of divine joy
amidst the seriousness of the day.

DIVINE SERVICES

THE WHOLE DAY OF YOM KIPPUR IS SPENT AT THE SYNA-GOGUE IN MEDITATION AND PRAYER

In ancient times the Service of the Day of Atonement
was very elaborate and impressive. It was only on Yom
Kippur that the High Priest entered the Holy of Holies,
the innermost part of the sanctuary, and offered sacrifices
for the redemption of his people. Since the destruction
of the Temple, prayer has taken the place of sacrifice,
and the whole day of Yom Kippur is spent in meditation
and prayer. Synagogues everywhere are thronged with
worshipers whose devotion and fervor are evidence of
the importance of the Day and of its hold upon the

Jewish soul. The order of Services on Yom Kippur is as follows:

Kol Nidre. The Maariv Service, on Yom Kippur eve, is called the Kol Nidre Service because the first prayer begins with the words, "Kol Nidre." The Kol Nidre prayer, in which we petition God to release us from all vows and commitments, has been a part of our ritual since the days of the Gaonim (about 800 C. E.). It was most fervently prayed, in the days of the Spanish Inquisition, by the Marranoes who openly pledged allegiance to the Church but secretly remained loyal to the faith of their fathers. Though a subject of controversial opinions, the Kol Nidre prayer, as a part of the Yom Kippur ritual, has retained its important position and its beautiful, traditional melody became universally known.

Shacharis. The Morning Service, called Shacharis, is a lengthy series of remorseful supplications. After the Shacharis, a lengthy portion of the Torah is read (Lev. 16) containing many ordinances for the observance of Yom Kippur and describing the ancient ceremony centered around the scapegoat, the order of sacrifices in the Temple, and the functions of the High Priest on that day. The Haphtorah is that famous sermon in which Isaiah gives his version on the purposes of the fast day. The Yizkor Memorial Service is usually held after the Shacharis, but in some congregations it is conducted later in the day.

Mussaf. The additional Service, or Mussaf, is a beautiful collection of penitential prayers. One of its features is the "Avodah," the description of the High Priest's functions in the Temple and of his solemn entry into the Holy of Holies. Another significant part of the Mussaf liturgy is the narrative of the ten martyrs who were tortured to death during the Bar Kochba revolution against the Roman Emperor Hadrian (132 C. E.).

Minchah, the afternoon Service. A short portion of the Torah is read and only three men are "called up." The Book of Jonah, telling how God performed an unusual miracle in order to bring His message of salvation through repentance to the people of Nineveh, is read as the Haphtorah for Minchah.

Neilah, the concluding Service. As the Neilah Service progresses, night gradually approaches and, according to Jewish tradition, the gates of heaven close and the fate of every Jew is sealed. At the conclusion of the Service, the "Sh'ma Yisroel" is proclaimed aloud, and the Shofar is blown to announce the end of the holy day.

NOTES ON YOM KIPPUR

(For Advanced Students and Adult Study Groups)

A day or two before Yom Kippur the ceremony of "Kapporos" is performed by observant Jews. A rooster (for a male) or a hen (for a female) is circled around the head with the words, "May this bird be a substitute for my life." This is in accordance with the ancient ritual of sacrifice in which the animal, or bird, was offered as a substitute for the life of the sinner. The "Kappoross" ceremony may also be performed with money which is afterwards given to a charitable cause.

Some of our rigidly orthodox brethren allow themselves to be flogged on Erev Yom Kippur as a symbol of penitence. Thirty-nine "Malkos" (floggings are administered in accordance with the punishment meted out to culprits in biblical days.

It is a tradition in Israel for the father to bless his children on Erev Yom Kippur.

The wearing of shoes, a luxury in olden days, was forbidden on Yom Kippur by the rabbis of the Talmud, hence the prevailing custom, in some synagogues, of removing footwear.

Many devout Jews spend the whole night of Yom Kippur repeating prayers, studying the Torah, and reciting Psalms.

The story of Jonah, though often doubted and even ridiculed, assumes special significance on Yom Kippur when we consider the message of the prophet which describes God as merciful and forgiving.

Fasting on Yom Kippur is not obligatory for people in poor health, nor for children below thirteen, the age of religious majority.

White, which symbolizes purity, is the predominant color of the Day of Atonement.

It is a custom in Israel to burn candles all day Yom Kippur in memory of the souls of the departed.

8. PASSOVER

Date and Duration

Passover is the first of the three "pilgrimage" festivals,
known in Hebrew as "Shalosh Regolim" (Passover,
Shavuos, Succos). The first two and the last two days of
the festival are Holy Days; the four intermediate days
are called "Chol Hammoed" or semi-holidays.

Names

THE FESTIVAL IS KNOWN AS "PESSACH," "CHAG HAMAT-
ZOS," "Z'MAN CHERUSSEINU," "CHAG HA-AVIV"

a. "Pessach," or Passover, is derived from the biblical
   narrative in which we are told that the angel of
   death "passed over" the homes of the Israelites
   when he killed the first-born of the Egyptians.
b. "Chag Hamatzos," the festival of unleavened
   bread, has become a name for the holiday because
   Matzos are eaten through the entire period of its
   observance.
c. "Z'man Cherusseinu," the festival of our freedom,
   is a popular name of Passover since its celebration
   marks the anniversary of the freedom of our ancestors and their Exodus from Egypt.
d. "Chag Ha-aviv," the spring festival, is another
   name given to Passover because it occurs in the
   spring of the year. It has an agricultural meaning,
   too, because our ancestors in Palestine connected

it with a harvest of minor importance and brought to the Temple in Jerusalem, as their pilgrimage offering, an Omer (pail) of the first ripe barley.

HISTORIC SIGNIFICANCE

PASSOVER COMMEMORATES THE BIRTH OF THE HEBREW NATION

As told in the Bible, the Exodus from Egypt, under the leadership of Moses, marks the first milestone in the history of our people. Through a series of miraculous events God gave freedom to an obscure group of Hebrew slaves and prepared them to receive the Torah and to proclaim the theory of monotheism to the people of the world. Every one of our three festivals has a historic background, but Passover is the key to the history of Israel, for every event in the subsequent history of our people dates back to the "Exodus," and every festival is a "Zecher litzias Mitzrayim," a remembrance of the going out from Egypt.

THE SEDER

THE MOST IMPORTANT FEATURE OF PASSOVER IS THE SEDER CEREMONY

The Seder, observed on the first and second nights of the festival, is the outstanding religious ceremony performed in the Jewish home. The word "seder" means "order" or "program," and the entire celebration is carried out in accordance with a set program established by tradition. The head of the family acts as the leader and usually occupies a seat in the center of the table. In front of him is a platter containing the following:

a. *Matzoh,* the unleavened bread, which reminds us

of the food eaten by our ancestors immediately after their departure from Egypt. Told to leave in haste, they took with them only unleavened dough which was later flattened into thin wafers and baked in the sun. This food sustained them before the "Manna" came to their rescue.

b. *Karpas,* parsley or celery dipped in salt water. This is an oriental type of appetizer to begin the meal with, but some commentators tell us that the parsley and salt water symbolize the hyssop and blood used by our ancestors in marking the doorposts of their houses.

c. *Moror,* bitter herbs, symbolizing the bitter life of slavery endured by our ancestors in Egypt.

d. *Charoses,* a mixture of apples, nuts, spices and wine, resembling the mortar from which our ancestors made bricks for the Pharaohs of Egypt.

e. *Z'roa,* a shank bone, symbolic of the paschal lamb which was slaughtered by the Israelites prior to their Exodus from Egypt.

f. *A roasted egg,* a remembrance of the Chagigah, the special peace offering made in the Temple in connection with this festival.

g. *Wine,* the drink "which causeth God and man to rejoice," lends a festive spirit to the festival of freedom. Red wine is preferable.

h. *Elijah's cup,* a special goblet of wine reserved for the prophet Elijah, the traditional forerunner of the Messiah.

FUNCTIONS AT THE SEDER

1. One member of the family acts as the "Leader" at Seder table. In many countries he is dressed in

pure white and is seated on a cushioned chair resembling a throne.

2. Each person at the Seder table is required to drink four cups of wine, commemorating the four different terms used by God in connection with the Exodus: "I shall redeem them," "I shall take them out," "I shall save them," "I shall take them unto me."

3. We dip the parsley into salt water and eat it as an appetizer.

4. We drink the wine in a reclining or relaxed position, with an air of freedom and a sense of security, thus showing our faith in the fulfillment of God's promise to be the guardian of Israel.

5. The middle one of the three Matzos, placed before the "Leader," is broken in two parts; one half is used for the "Hammotzi," opening the meal; the other half is the "Afikomon," eaten at the conclusion of the meal.

6. The youngest member of the family asks the "four questions," and the entire ceremony of the Seder is a series of answers to these questions.

7. We recite the Hagadah, the special book which contains the ritual of the Seder.

8. We eat the Matzoh after pronouncing a special "Brochoh" over it.

9. The Moror is dipped into the Charosses and the two eaten together.

10. During that part of the program when we bid defiance to our oppressors we open the door to welcome in the courageous spirit of the prophet Elijah.

11. We conclude the meal with the eating of the "Afi-

komon," that piece of Matzoh which was set aside as the "dessert." The "Afikomon" is usually hidden in order to make certain it will be available when it is called for in the "Seder" of the evening.

12. We recite many psalms and sing many songs, concluding with the "Chad Gadya" (one kid, one kid), a legendary tale to which many allegorical interpretations have been given.

13. On the Seder evening we are all equal, all free. Servants eat at the table together with their masters.

DIVINE SERVICES

Although Passover is primarily observed in the home, there is an elaborate ritual prescribed for the Services in the synagogue. Before the Seder ceremony a short Maariv Service is recited. The morning Service consists of (a) the Shacharis, (b) the Hallel, (c) the reading of the Torah and Haphtorah, (d) the sermon or scripture interpretation, (e) the Mussaf Service.

On the first day of Passover a special prayer for "dew," known as "Tal," is recited. On the Sabbath of Chol Hammoed the "Song of Songs" is read, and the Haphtorah of the day is the dramatic story of Ezekiel's vision of the dry bones. On the seventh day we read the biblical description of the miraculous crossing of the Red Sea; on the last day we recite the Yizkor Memorial Service.

HOLIDAY REST

All forms of manual labor which are forbidden on the Sabbath are also forbidden on the first two days and the last two days of the Passover, and only work essential to the preparation of food is permitted. We are allowed, though with certain restrictions, to work on the four intermediate days. (Chol Hammoed.)

SPECIAL FOOD

During the week of Passover the observant Jew eats special foods that are "Kosher L'Pessach," kosher for the Passover use. He abstains not only from bread, but also from cereals, beans and all types of food that were cooked, or processed, for the general use, not for Passover. The dietary laws for Passover call for special dishes and utensils to be used during the week of the festival.

NOTES ON PASSOVER

(For Advanced Students and Adult Study Groups)

It is customary in many Jewish communities to collect a Passover relief fund, known as "Mo'os Chittim," and to supply the needy of the community with Passover food.

The word "Chometz" (literally "leavened") was originally applied to bread, but now it is a general name for all food articles that are ritually unfit for Passover use.

"M'chiras Chometz," the "selling of the leaven," is a unique transaction designed to circumvent the law which prohibits the Jew from possessing Chometz during the Passover week. Two or three days before Passover the observant Jew sells his Chometz to the rabbi who, in turn, sells it to a non-Jew and then buys it back from him at the end of the holiday.

"B'dikas Chometz," the "searching for leaven," is a ceremony performed on the night before Passover.

"Bi-ur Chometz," the "burning of leaven," is another

ceremony on the morning of Erev Pessach. It indicates
that every kind of Chometz has been removed from the
home before the week of Passover.

The Pidyon Habben, the ceremony of redeeming the
first-born males from the Cohen, has its origin in the
Passover story. When God smote the first-born of Egypt
and saved those of Israel, He ordained that every Jewish
first-born (B'chor) be the symbolical property of the
Cohen until redeemed for a certain consideration.

Because the first-born of the Egyptians were killed and
the first-born of the Hebrews were spared, every Jewish
B'chor is conscious of his debt of gratitude to God. Tradition has designated the day before Passover as a fast
day for every B'chor, but this fast may be broken to participate in a religious feast, such as a "Siyum" (concluding the study of a tractate of the Talmud), a Bris Milah,
a Pidyon Habben, or a wedding.

The lamb which our ancestors slaughtered prior to
their departure from Egypt has assumed historic importance as the "Pessach" or "Paschal" lamb. It was offered
as an annual sacrifice, on the day before Passover, in the
period of the first Temple and also in the days of the
second Temple. Many symbols of the paschal lamb have
been retained to this day and incorporated in the ritual
of the Seder.

It is a source of regret, both to the synagogue and to
the church, that the blood of the paschal lamb forms the
basis of an atrocious libel against the Jewish people,
that falsehood known as the "Blood Accusation."

Christianity traces its origin to the historic observance
of Passover. The Mohammedans also observe a Passover,
known as "Nabi Musa," the festival in honor of the
prophet Moses.

The few remaining Samaritans (descendants of the Lost Ten Tribes) still perform the ancient ritual of slaughtering a paschal lamb on the evening of Passover. This is done on the top of Mt. Gerizim, overlooking the biblical town of Shechem, or Nablus.

The three Matzos which are placed in front of the "Leader" at the Seder table are symbolic of the three classes of Jews—Cohen, Levi, Israel.

When we mention the ten plagues inflicted upon the Egyptians, we remove ten drops of wine from the cup in front of us, as an indication that our cup of joy is not full when we think of suffering humanity.

Passover warns us against every form of tyranny, oppression or injustice. Many ethical laws of the Mosaic legislation are supplemented with the words, "Remember that you were once slaves in the land of Egypt."

We observe two festive days in the beginning of the holiday and also two days at its conclusion, while in Palestine only one day is observed at the beginning and one at the end. The source of the two-day observance dates back to the early days when our people started each month at the appearance of the new moon and were thus uncertain as to the exact day of the festival. It has also been suggested that while some Jews were observing the holiday in one part of the world, others were not, because of the variation in time in different parts of the globe. A two-day observance was therefore introduced and became a tradition to the Jewish people outside of Palestine, in all lands of the exile. This explanation may also be applied to the other two festivals—Shavuos and Succos.

9. SHAVUOS

SHAVUOS, OR SHABUOTH, OCCURS ON THE SIXTH AND
SEVENTH DAYS OF SIVAN

It is the second of the three pilgrimage festivals (Passover, Shavuos, and Succos), but unlike the other two
festivals is observed for only two days.

NAMES

SHAVUOS IS KNOWN AS "FEAST OF WEEKS," "PENTECOST,"
"CHAG HABIKURIM," "Z'MAN MATTAN TOROSSEINU"

(a) The name Feast of Weeks is given to the festival
because it comes seven weeks after Passover.

(b) It is called "Pentecost" (Greek for "fiftieth") because it comes on the fiftieth day after counting
forty-nine days, or seven weeks.

(c) "Chag Habikurim" means the Feast of the First
Fruit. On this festival our ancestors came from all
parts of Palestine into the Temple at Jerusalem,
bringing offerings of the first ripe fruit.

(d) "Z'man Mattan Torosseinu," the festival which
marks the anniversary of the giving of our Torah,
is the traditional connotation of Shavuos, though
the Bible does not directly connect this festival
with the giving of the Torah.

HISTORICAL REASON

SHEVUOSS COMMEMORATES THE BIRTH OF JUDAISM

Our religion, based on monotheism, had its birth at Mt. Sinai when the ten commandments were given to our ancestors. These commandments, God's gift to Israel, became in turn Israel's gift to humanity and the foundation of most moral and civil laws.

AGRICULTURAL SIGNIFICANCE

SHAVUOS, AS THE "CHAG HABIKURIM," WAS PALESTINE'S FESTIVAL OF THE FIRST RIPE FRUIT

Offering the "first" to God was an oriental custom even before the days of Sinai. The first child, the first male animal, the first corn, and the first fruit were always offered by orientals, Jew and pagan alike, to the god of nature, whatever the deity or the form in which he was worshiped. In the Torah the offering of Bikurim was ordered by God, and our people observed this holiday as a festive occasion of great significance. Even today flowers and green foliage, the gifts of nature, are used profusely to decorate the synagogue on Shevuoss.

CONFIRMATION

SHEVUOSS IS ALSO KNOWN AS THE FESTIVAL OF CONFIRMATION

Modern synagogues, conservative and reform, celebrate the ceremony of confirmation on Shevuoss. In the first place, the confirmation service re-enacts the event of Mt. Sinai, for our children, like our ancestors, accept the faith of Israel with the words, "We shall do and obey." Second, we bring to God on that day, as did our ancestors before us, the first ripe fruit of our religious schools.

SERVICES

THE SERVICES ON SHAVUOS FOLLOW THE RITUAL PRE-
SCRIBED FOR THE THREE FESTIVALS

The reading of the Torah, on the first day of the holiday, is from the book of Exodus and tells the events
which took place at the foot of Mt. Sinai. The Haphtorah
is the first chapter of Ezekiel, describing the prophet's
vision and his first glimpse of God. In addition to the
portion of the Torah and the Haphtorah, the "Book of
Ruth" is read on the first day of Shavuos because it tells
how a Gentile woman (Ruth) accepted the Jewish faith
and also because its story has a harvest scene as background.

FOOD

There is no special food prescribed for Shavuos. However, it is customary to eat dishes made of dairy products.
In the first place, the festival occurs in the summer season of the year when milk is plentiful; second, the Torah,
according to the Talmud, is like "milk and honey";
third, there is the influence of an acrostic based on the
words, "*M*incha *CH*adasha *L*adonoi *B*'shovuosseichem"
(bring an offering unto God on Shavuos), the first four
letters of which make up the word M'CHLB, food made
of milk.

NOTES ON SHAVUOS

(For Advanced Students and Adult Study Groups)

The forty-nine days between Passover and Shavuos
are counted, and these seven weeks are known as the
S'FIRA (counting) period. When our ancestors lived in

Palestine, each pilgrim was required to bring an "Omer" (pail) of barley to the Temple on the second day of Passover, and the days following the "Omer" were counted until Shavuos, as ordered in the Torah (Lev. 23:15). The custom of counting these forty-nine days (S'fira) has been an unbroken tradition in Israel to this day.

In the Bar Kochba revolution against Rome (132 C. E.) Rabbi Akiba's pupils were almost annihilated by the Roman legions and by the plague during the S'fira days. On the thirty-third day of the Omer (Lag B'omer) they scored a victory and also the plague ceased. Since then, the S'fira days are sad ones in Israel; no weddings or joyous celebrations are held in that period except for Lag B'omer which is celebrated with considerable festivity, especially by school children.

Tradition has it that King David was born, and also died, on Shavuos. It is therefore customary in many orthodox circles to recite psalms on Shavuos in honor of the "Sweet Singer of Israel."

A Cabalistic arrangement of special readings, known as "Tikun shell Shavuos," is recited on the first night of the festival. Many observant Jews stay awake all night, reciting excerpts from the Torah, the Prophets, and the Talmud. Legend has it that during that night the heavens open up for a single moment and all petitions uttered during that moment are promptly granted.

Modern Palestine has revived the ceremony of "Bikurim." Once a year the Jewish farmers of Palestine, especially of the Emek, gather in Haifa and stage a modern version of the Chag Habikurim. Young people dressed in white march in procession and carry the products of the orchards and fields. The fruits and vegetables are then sold and the proceeds given to the Jewish National Fund.

LINCOLN BIBLE INSTITUTE

10. SUCCOS

Date and Duration

SUCCOS, OR SUCCOTH, OCCURS ON THE FIFTEENTH DAY OF TISHRI AND LASTS FOR NINE DAYS

Succos is the third of the three pilgrimage festivals. The first two days and the last two days of the festival are holy days, while the five intermediate days are called Chol Hammoed, semi-holidays.

Names

SUCCOS IS KNOWN AS "FEAST OF BOOTHS," "FEAST OF TABERNACLES," "CHAG HAASIF," "Z'MAN SIMCHOSSEINU"

(a) The "Succah" (booth) is the main symbol of the holiday. The Feast of "Succos" (the plural of "Succah"), is therefore translated as the Feast of Booths.

(b) The "Tabernacle" was the collapsible tent used as a sanctuary in the wilderness. The festival of tents (Succos) is therefore called the Feast of Tabernacles.

(c) "Chag Haasif" (Harvest Festival) is a name frequently used in the Bible for Succos, the week of the year in which the Jewish people of Palestine expressed their gratitude to God for the harvest.

(d) "Z'man Simchosseinu" (Season of Rejoicing). Of the three festivals, Succos is the only one on which the Jew was told to rejoice and be happy—"V'somachto B'chagecho," "thou shalt rejoice with thy festival" (Deut. 16:14).

HISTORIC REASON

THE SUCCAH SYMBOLIZES THE PERIOD OF THE WILDERNESS

Just as we were told to eat Matzos to remember the food which our ancestors ate after their hasty departure from Egypt, so were we ordered by God to dwell in temporary huts, or Succahs, as a reminder of the tents in which our ancestors dwelt during the forty years of their wanderings in the wilderness. "Ye shall dwell in booths seven days: all that are home-born in Israel shall dwell in booths; that your future generations may know that I made the children of Israel to dwell in booths, when I brought them out of the land of Egypt; I am the Lord your God" (Lev. 24:42).

The Succah is a temporary dwelling, or shelter, without a permanent roof. Its top covering usually consists of pine or hemlock branches which are laid on lightly so that the sky is visible through them. The Succah is decorated with flowers, foliage, and with products of the field and of the orchard.

AGRICULTURAL REASON

Succos is the annual Harvest Festival, observed by our ancestors with joy and song and good-will offerings. We retain the traditional significance of this holiday even though exiled from our land and even though we have been an urban people for many centuries.

HARVEST SYMBOLS

We bring into the synagogue, and into the Succah, four species which symbolize the harvest. They are:

1. *Esrog,* a citrus fruit, possibly the most highly val-

ued fruit of the orient because of its health-giving qualities;

2. *Lulav,* a branch of the palm tree, which is waved in all directions to symbolize the decorative effects of the harvest scene;

3. *Hadassim,* myrtle twigs, used because of their small leaves and fine aroma, and because they retain their green color long after they are cut;

4. *Arovoth,* willows of the brook, to represent the lowly bushes and fruitless trees.

With these in our hands we march around the reading desk of the synagogue, reciting the Hallel and singing Hosannahs. Every morning, for seven days (except on the Sabbath), a benediction is pronounced over the Lulav.

Hoshanah Rabbah, the seventh day of Succos, is a solemn day. According to tradition, the fate of each Jew, which is written down on Rosh Hashanah and sealed on Yom Kippur, is sealed with finality (G'mar Ch'simah) on Hoshanah Rabbah. Many observant Jews spend the preceding evening in devotional exercises.

Sh'mini Atzeres. The eighth day of the holiday is called Sh'mini Atzeres, the eighth day of Solemn Assembly. On that day the Yizkor Memorial prayer is recited in addition to the regular holiday Services. As the rainy season in Palestine commenced around this time of year, it was customary to recite a special prayer for rain, called "Geshem," and this custom has been retained to this day. The "Geshem" prayer is recited, on Sh'mini Atzeres, with great solemnity.

Simchas Torah. The ninth day of the festival is Simchas Torah, the day of "rejoicing with the Torah." On that day we finish the cycle of the reading of the Torah and then begin it over again. All the scrolls of the Torah are taken from the Holy Ark and are carried in a procession (Hakofos) through the aisles of the synagogue. Children carrying small flags or lighted torches join in the procession. The observance of the day, universally joyous, varies in different parts of the world, but eating, drinking, and dancing are universal characteristics of Simchas Torah.

Services. The regular holiday Services, as traditionally arranged for the three festivals, are followed on Succos. "Ecclesiastes," or "Koheleth," the biblical book of religious philosophy, chiefly pessimistic, is read on the Sabbath of Chol Hammoed. This may be due to the fact that at this time of year the approaching autumn season presages the death of nature.

NOTES ON SUCCOS

(For Advanced Students and Adult Study Groups)

The frail, roofless Succah is the symbol of God's protection, both past and present, to the people of Israel.

The Succah is also symbolic of the "clouds of glory" with which God shielded Israel from harm in the wilderness.

According to the Talmud, the Succah is to have more shade than sunshine, perhaps as a symbol of Jewish life in many parts of the world.

The building of the Succah is begun right after the fast of Yom Kippur, in keeping with the saying, "They shall go from strength to strength."

In addition to the harvest, water is the most essential element in sustaining life. In ancient Palestine the

"Festivity at the Drinking Well" (Simchath Beth Ha-shoevoh), usually held on Chol Hammoed of Succos, was the most joyous ceremony of the festival. That unique ceremony has been resumed in modern Palestine, and in many parts of the Jewish world celebrations are still arranged in honor of that ancient festivity.

There is no special food prescribed or traditionally adopted for Succos, but newly harvested foods are enjoyed through the week of the festival.

Our custom of uttering a "Brochoh," an expression of gratitude, for everything that we eat or drink may have its origin in the prayers which our ancestors recited in the celebration of the harvest festival.

It has repeatedly been stated that the establishment of the American feast of Thanksgiving was influenced by the biblical harvest festival of Succos.

11. CHANUKAH

DATE AND DURATION

CHANUKAH, OR HANUKAH, OCCURS ON THE TWENTY-FIFTH
DAY OF KISLEV AND LASTS FOR EIGHT DAYS

MINOR FESTIVAL

CHANUKAH IS ONE OF OUR TWO MINOR FESTIVALS (CHA-
NUKAH AND PURIM)

Unlike the Sabbath and the holidays, the observance
of Chanukah was not ordained by God through Moses
but was agreed upon by the Jewish people themselves.
Therefore, manual labor may be performed during its
eight days.

NAME

CHANUKAH MEANS "DEDICATION"

It commemorates the day on which the second Temple
at Jerusalem was re-dedicated to the service of God after
having been desecrated by the Syrians and used for idola-
trous worship. That event of re-dedication remained a
memorable one in the annals of Jewish history.

JUDAISM VS. HELLENISM

CHANUKAH MARKS A VICTORY OF JUDAISM OVER HELLEN-
ISM

Hellenism was the collective name for the Greek culture of antiquity. Its language, philosophy, gods, arts,
athletic games, and dances were a complete civilization

in pre-Christian days. When Alexander the Great annexed Palestine to his vast empire (in the year 332 B. C. E.), he prepared the way for the entrance of Hellenism into the Holy Land. Later, in the year 250 B. C. E., the Septuagint, the Greek translation of the Bible, was introduced to the people of Palestine, bringing, according to the Talmud, great consternation to the faithful Jews, but great rejoicing among the Hellenized Jews who participated in Greek culture and even worshiped Greek idols. Hellenism was a culture of aesthetic living, of beauty and grace; Judaism was a religion of holy living, of justice and peace. There was a constant struggle between the two cultures, and the story of Chanukah records the triumph of Judaism over Hellenism.

THE HISTORY

THE STORY OF CHANUKAH IS ONE OF THE IMPORTANT CHAPTERS IN THE HISTORY OF THE JEWISH PEOPLE

In the days of the second Temple, in the year 202 B. C. E., Palestine came under the rule of the Hellenistic Syrians. In the year 175 B. C. E. Antiochus ascended the throne of Syria, and he announced his intention of suppressing the laws and customs of Judaism and forcing Hellenism upon the Jewish people. Any adherence to Jewish law or tradition was forbidden under penalty of death. Many Jews accepted the order, but the pious Jews, known as Chassidim, resisted. In the year 168 B. C. E. the aged priest Mattathias, of the Hasmonean family, raised a revolt against Hellenism and, using the slogan of Moses, "Those who are for God, follow me!" gathered an army of faithful defenders of Judaism. His son Judah Maccabeus, or Maccabee, soon took command of the small army and offered battle to the superior forces of Antiochus. It was a "Holy War" in the full sense of the word, for the Syrians were determined not only to annihilate the Jewish people but also to exterminate every vestige of the Jewish faith. Maccabee and his followers fought furiously, and after a desperate struggle, lasting for three years, subdued the enemy and recaptured the city of Jerusalem.

THE VICTORY

JUDAH CLEANSED THE TEMPLE AND RE-DEDICATED IT TO THE SERVICE OF GOD

The Temple had been turned into a center of Greek idolatry, where pagan ceremonies and immoral orgies were held, and a large statue of Zeus, the Greek god, had been placed in front of the Holy of Holies. Maccabee removed all the ceremonial objects identified with Hellenism and put in their place the vessels and the symbols of Judaism. A public Festival of Dedication (Chanukah) was held on the twenty-fifth day of Kislev (165 B. C. E.).

THE MIRACLE

THE CEREMONY OF DEDICATION WAS AUGMENTED THROUGH THE MIRACLE OF THE OIL

Legend tells us that at the ceremony of the re-dedication of the Temple a cruse of consecrated oil, enough for only one day, was found. The Ner Tamid, the perpetual lamp, was kindled and the small amount of oil miraculously lasted for eight days. This is why Chanukah is observed for this length of time.

Festival of Light

CHANUKAH IS OFTEN DESIGNATED AS THE FESTIVAL OF
LIGHT

The main feature of Chanukah is the kindling of
lights, lit because of the miracle of the oil and also because the Torah, "the light of Israel," was saved in the
Maccabean victory. We kindle one candle on the first
night and increase the number every night until eight
candles are lit on the last night.

Al Hanissim

In addition to the regular week-day Service, Hallel is
recited every morning, and a portion of the Torah is
read. "Al Hanissim," a prayer of gratitude for the miracles wrought in behalf of our ancestors, is recited during the week at every Service and at "Grace" after meals.

Home Observances

Chanukah is primarily a home festival. "Latkes," a
favorite food among Eastern European Jews, has become
a popular Chanukah food in many parts of the world.
The game with the spinning top, known as the "Dreidel,"
or "Trendel," has become symbolic of the holiday. In
the Middle Ages the Jewish people frowned upon games
because they consumed valuable time that should be devoted to the study of the Torah, but on Chanukah they
recommended the game of chess because its military tac-
tics symbolized the strategy of Judah Maccabee.

NOTES ON CHANUKAH

(For Advanced Students and Adult Study Groups)

The history of Chanukah is *not* recorded in the Bible. It is to be found in Maccabees I and Maccabees II, in the "Apocrypha," a set of books that were either not accepted in the Bible collection or were written after the Old Testament had been closed.

It is hard to imagine what might have happened if our ancestors had lost in their struggle against Hellenism. It is reasonably certain, however, that in such an eventuality none of the monotheistic religions—Judaism, Christianity, Mohammedanism—would have been in existence today.

History tells us that the early Christians in Antioch, Syria, used to celebrate the Feast of the Maccabees.

Chanukah is a very important festival because it celebrates an historic event in which both the Jewish religion and the Jewish nation were saved.

The Zionist movement, striving to re-establish the Jewish nation in Palestine, has placed great significance on the observance of Chanukah because of its importance in the history of the Jewish nation.

Chanukah is the only festive season which commemorates a Jewish victory on the field of battle.

The word "Maccabee" is now frequently used, in Palestine and elsewhere, for Jewish military or athletic organizations. When Jewish soldiers, in all parts of the world, are praised for acts of bravery, they are often spoken of as heroic Maccabees.

The Talmudic story of the martyred Hannah and her

seven sons reveal the spirit of heroism and self-sacrifice which prevailed among our ancestors in that period of stubborn resistance against Hellenism.

The Talmud tells us that according to a ruling of the school of Hillel the number of Chanukah lights is increased every night because the miracle of the oil increased in importance as the light continued to burn for eight days.

Chanukah is not a holiday for the exchange of gifts, yet children are given what is usually known as "Chanukah gelt."

Many poems, stage plays, and oratorios have been written around the story of Chanukah. "Judah Maccabeus" by Longfellow and "The Banner of the Jew" by Emma Lazarus are the outstanding American examples.

Chanukah menorahs, of all types and design, are found throughout the world. They are important in the history of Jewish religious art.

12. PURIM

DATE AND DURATION

PURIM OCCURS ON THE FOURTEENTH DAY OF ADAR AND IS
OBSERVED FOR ONLY ONE DAY

MINOR FESTIVAL

PURIM IS ONE OF OUR TWO MINOR FESTIVALS (PURIM AND
CHANUKAH)

Unlike the Sabbath and the holidays, the observance
of Purim was not ordained by God through Moses but
was proclaimed through an edict issued by Mordecai and
Esther. Therefore, manual labor is permitted on Purim.

NAME

PURIM MEANS "FEAST OF LOTS"

Haman cast lots (Purim) to determine the day on
which to destroy the Jewish people and decided upon
the thirteenth day of Adar. When his scheme was frustrated, the Jewish people decided to celebrate the following day, the fourteenth of Adar, to commemorate their
deliverance from the fateful "Purim."

DAY OF HAPPINESS

PURIM IS THE HAPPIEST DAY IN THE JEWISH CALENDAR

On Purim we celebrate the survival of the Jewish people as told in the "Book of Esther" in a series of dramatic
events. Ahashverosh, King of Persia, sent away his queen,
Vashti, and made Esther, a Jewish maiden, his queen.

Haman, an arch-enemy of Israel, became Prime Minister. Every citizen of the land knelt before him except Mordecai, the cousin of Esther, who refused to kneel before a descendant of Amalek. Haman, because of his hatred for Mordecai, secured the king's consent to exterminate the Jews. Esther, however, risked her life and appeared before the king, though uninvited, to plead for her people. Her plea was heeded, Haman was hanged, Mordecai was given Haman's post as Prime Minister, and the Jewish people were saved.

THE MEGILLAH

THE BOOK OF ESTHER, KNOWN AS THE "MEGILLAH," IS READ ON THE EVENING AND ON THE MORNING OF PURIM

The reading of the Megillah has become an important part of the observance of Purim. Jewish law even goes so far as to make it obligatory upon every Jewish person to listen to the reading of the Megillah.

FOOD

"HOMON TASH," A TRIANGULAR CAKE, IS A SPECIAL FOOD TRADITIONALLY CONNECTED WITH PURIM

Many interpretations have been given to the "Homon Tash." Some claim that it resembles Haman's ears; others that it represents Haman's triangular hat; still others trace its origin to the Hebrew word "tash" (weakened), for Haman weakened when he heard the decree issued against him.

Legend tells us that Queen Esther, while at the king's court, did not eat any food forbidden to the Jewish people, but lived on vegetables and seeds. Hence the use of poppy seeds in the "Homon Tash."

SHALACH MONOS

THE CUSTOM OF EXCHANGING GIFTS ON PURIM IS KNOWN
BY ITS HEBREW NAME, "SHALACH MONOS"

We read in the Megillah, "It shall be a day of feasting
and of gladness, of sending gifts one to another, and gifts
to the poor." Since giving gifts adds zest to every occasion, and giving alms gladdens the poor, Purim brings
happiness to us and comfort to our brethren in need.

NOTES ON PURIM

(For Advanced Students and Adult Study Groups)

The Book of Esther is the only book in the Bible in
which the name of God is not mentioned. It was incorporated into Holy Writ because the hand of God was
believed discernible in the miracle which resulted from
the king's sleepless night (Esther, Ch. 6).

The day before Purim is "Taanis Esther," a fast day
observed in honor of Queen Esther who fasted for three
days prior to her appearance before the king.

Our attitude toward Haman is of interest. We show
no resentment toward Pharaoh during the celebration
of Passover, nor do we curse the name of Antiochus during the week of Chanukah, but on Purim we show our
hatred for Haman whenever his name is mentioned during the reading of the Megillah. The following reasons
have been given for our eternal dislike of Haman:

(1) Haman was a coward and did not openly fight our
people. Mark his words to the king, "There is a
certain people . . . if it pleases the king, they

shall be destroyed." The Jewish people were not even mentioned by name.

(2) In our history our people have often been persecuted on religious grounds. With Haman, however, it was a case of sheer hatred, not based on opposing ideas nor on religious differences.

(3) Many of our enemies have oppressed us in order to confiscate our wealth or to gain economic advantages by eliminating us as competitors. Haman, however, did not seek profit through our destruction and even paid the vast sum of ten thousand talents of silver to satisfy his lust for blood.

(4) Haman's hatred was inhuman and unreasonable. He was ready to slaughter innocent people in order to revenge himself upon one individual.

Throughout Jewish history the people of Jewish communities have celebrated their own local Purims, commemorating days on which they were saved from their enemies.

Plays and skits are usually performed on Purim by amateur "Purim Shpielers" (or actors). Throughout the ages pious Jewish men disregarded the biblical prohibition against wearing women's garments, and on this day bearded Jews grotesquely attired themselves when they played the parts of Esther, Zeresh, or Vashti.

"Ad-lo-yada" is a state of extreme drunkenness permitted only on Purim. Palestinian Jews frequently stage "Ad-lo-yada" carnivals on Purim.

In case of a leap year, Purim is observed on the fourteenth day of the second Adar, while the fourteenth day of the first Adar is known as "Purim Kotton," a Purim of minor importance.

The day after Purim is called "Shushan Purim," the

additional day of joy observed by the people of Shushan, the Persian capital where the historic event took place. We observe this day to a small degree.

The Talmud tells us that many Jewish festivals may cease to exist, but Purim will always be observed. This assertion is based on the quotation, "The days of Purim shall not fail from among the Jews, nor the memorial of them perish from their seed" (Esther 9:28).

Esther's Hebrew name was Hadassah. The American Women's Zionist Organization, organized on Purim 1911, adopted the name of "Hadassah" in honor of the biblical heroine.

13. SPECIAL DAYS

(From Nissan Through Adar)

In addition to the holidays, there are several special days which are observed in Jewish life because of their religious or historic significance. They are:

1. ROSH CHODESH

The first day (or days) of each month is observed as a festive day, and the Hallel is recited at the morning Service. In some countries, the day is traditionally observed as a Jewish woman's holiday. A legend has it that the women in Israel refused to give their ornaments toward the making of the Golden Calf, and Jewish women were given this special day for rest and recreation as a reward.

2. LAG B'OMER

The thirty-third day in the S'fira period between Passover and Shavuos is universally observed as a school children's holiday. (See article on Shavuos.)

3. SHIVAH OSSOR B'TAMMUZ

The seventeenth day of Tammuz was designated as a fast day because on that day, in 586 B. C. E., the Babylonians entered the city of Jerusalem after a long siege. The period between the seventeenth day of Tammuz and the ninth of Ab is known as "the three sad weeks."

4. TISHA B'AB

The ninth of Ab is the Black Fast of the Jewish people. It is also spoken of as the national Jewish "Yahrzeit." The first Temple was destroyed on that day (586 B. C. E.), the second Temple was destroyed on that day (70 C. E.), and the last stronghold of Bar Kochba (Bethar) fell on that day (135 C. E.). In recent history, the expulsion of the Jews from Spain occurred on that day (1492 C. E.). Special Services are held in the synagogue; the "Lamentations" of Jeremiah are recited; and many "Kinnos," (dirges) written by Judah Halevy, Hakalir, and others are chanted to sad tunes.

5. TZOM GEDALIAH

The Fast of Gedaliah is observed on the day after Rosh Hashanah, the third of Tishri. The assassination of Gedaliah, governor of Jerusalem, soon after the destruction of the first Temple, was so catastrophic an event that the day on which it occurred was proclaimed a permanent fast day by the Jews who remained in Palestine.

6. ASSOROH B'TEBETH

The tenth of Tebeth has been designated as a minor fast day because on that day the Babylonian invaders broke through the outer defenses of Jerusalem (586 B. C. E.).

7. CHAMISHO OSSOR B'SHEVAT

The fifteenth day of Shevat has become known as the "Rosh Hashanah for Trees," or Jewish Arbor Day. Fruits of all kinds, preferably Palestinian, are eaten on that day. In modern Palestine the day is ceremoniously observed with hikes to the woods and by the planting of trees.

8. Taanis Esther

We fast on the thirteenth day of Adar, the day before Purim, just as Esther did prior to her appearing before the king. The heroine of Purim is immortalized in Israel through the observance of a fast day in her honor.

14. JEWISH DIETARY LAWS

Jewish ceremonial life includes a series of dietary laws. The commandment, "Thou shalt not eat any abominable thing" (Deut. 14:3), restrains the Jewish person from eating anything forbidden by the dietary laws of Judaism. Destined to be a "holy people," we were given a series of laws to regulate our diet and to discipline our physical desires in accordance with the will of God.

"The dietary laws," says Maimonides, "train us in the mastery over our appetites; they accustom us to restrain the growth of desire, the indulgence in seeking that which is pleasant, and the disposition to consider the pleasure of eating and drinking as the end of man's existence." In Leviticus, chapter 11, and in Deuteronomy, chapter 14, the Jewish people were given a series of dietary laws which have been retained to this day as an important part of Jewish life. The following is a summary of our dietary laws as ordained in the Torah, modified in the Talmud, and codified in the Shulchan Aruch. (See Part 5, Ch. 3.)

KOSHER AND TRAIFA

All foods that can be eaten in accordance with Jewish dietary laws are *kosher,* while all foods ritually forbidden to the Jewish people are *traifa.* "Kashruth," or "Kashrus," is the collective name for the many laws pertaining to kosher food.

Animals

Animals that are cloven-hoofed and chew the cud—cattle, sheep, goats, deer—are clean, or kosher. Animals that have neither or only one of these two characteristics —horse, camel, swine, hare—are unclean, or traifa. Carnivorous, or flesh eating, beasts are forbidden.

Fish

Only fish that have fins and scales are kosher, while fish that have only one or neither of the two characteristics are traifa. All kinds of shell fish, such as lobsters, shrimps, oysters, and clams are forbidden.

Birds

Domestic birds and those fowl that were used for sacrifices in the Temple are kosher. Wild birds of the forest and all birds of prey are forbidden.

Prohibition of Blood

THE USE OF BLOOD, EITHER AS A DRINK OR AS A PART OF FOOD, IS STRICTLY PROHIBITED

"Flesh with the life thereof, which is the blood, ye shall not eat" (Gen. 9:4). This order, given to the sons of Noah, is one of the first commands recorded in the Bible. Judaism maintains that man may kill an animal and eat its flesh because man is destined for a higher mission in life than the animal, but he must not eat the blood. "Blood is the life of the animal, don't eat the meat with the animal's life" (Deut. 12:23).

The ritual preparation of kosher meat calls, first of all, for the removal of all veins which contain blood. The meat is then soaked in water for half an hour, after which it is covered with salt, kept under salt for an hour, then thoroughly rinsed. Liver must be baked over an open fire in order to remove the abundance of blood from it.

SHECHITAH

FOR MEAT TO BE RITUALLY KOSHER, THE ANIMAL MUST BE KILLED BY A SPECIAL PROCESS KNOWN AS "SHECHITAH"

The ritual slaughtering of animals or birds, the "Shechitah," is performed by a *Shochet,* a learned and pious man who is specially trained for that work. The "Shechitah," performed with a prayer, is an operation in which the vital organs of the throat (windpipe and gullet) are slashed rapidly with an extremely sharp knife, and most of the blood escapes from the animal's body. All the parts and organs of the animal, especially the lungs, are then examined (B'dikah) and if no defects are found, the meat is declared kosher. Animals not slaughtered in accordance with the laws of "Shechitah" are termed "N'vailah," and their meat must not be eaten. The act of "Shechitah" is rapid and almost painless, and all objections to "Shechitah" on grounds of cruelty are baseless and false.

MILK AND MEAT

DAIRY PRODUCTS AND MEAT FOOD MUST NOT BE EATEN, NOR COOKED, TOGETHER

The prohibition against the using of meat and milk together is contained in the commandment, "Thou shalt not seethe the kid in its mother's milk," a phrase repeated three times in the Torah. Every mixture of milk and meat is forbidden, and the observant Jewish home has one set of utensils and dishes for meat and another for dairy food. After eating meat products there is a waiting period before milk food can be eaten, its length varies from six hours in some countries to a shorter period in others. Foods prepared with meat are known as "fleishig," those derived from milk are "milchig"; foods that are prepared with neither milk nor meat are called "parveh." Fish, eggs, fruits and vegetables may be eaten with either meat or milk.

HINDQUARTERS

THE MEAT OF THE HINDQUARTERS IS NOT EATEN BY THE OBSERVANT JEW

The hindquarters of cattle are not eaten unless the fat and the sinew of the thigh-vein are removed (porged), a process that is ordinarily not performed because it is both difficult and wasteful. We refrain from eating the meat of the hindquarters in conformity with a prohibition which dates back to Jacob's struggle with the angel, an incident from which the patriarch came out limping but proud of the acquisition of the name of "Israel." "The children of Israel shall not eat the sinew of the thigh-vein which is upon the hollow of the thigh, unto this day" (Gen. 32:33).

NOTES ON DIETARY LAWS

(For Advanced Students and Adult Study Groups)

The word "kosher" is often interpreted as "clean," but it actually means "ritually fit." Many foods may be perfectly clean, yet not kosher.

Dietary laws have been a fence around the Jewish home and have made it a place where religion is not merely discussed but actually lived. With the observance of these laws the Jewish home becomes "a sanctuary in miniature."

Food determines the ethnic characteristics of many a people. In our case, dietary regulations have not only added distinctiveness to our people but also served to remind us of the Sabbath, of the festivals, and of many historic occasions.

The Talmud speaks of the dietary laws as a social barrier against assimilation. "If you eat the meat of the pagan, you will also drink his wine, and finally you will marry his daughter (Sabbath 17).

The absurdity of the "Blood Accusation" (use of blood with the Passover ritual) is especially evident from the fact that the Jewish people, throughout the ages, have been strict abstainers from the use of blood in any form whatsoever.

The sport of hunting has never been popular with the Jewish people. In the first place, the Jew has an aversion to killing for sport's sake; secondly, he cannot eat the meat of the bagged animal because it was not killed in accordance with the laws of "Shechitah."

The attitude of the Jewish people toward the dietary laws constitutes a barometer of the state of Judaism. When Judaism is observed in its entirety, the dietary laws form a natural part of Jewish life and their importance is neither questioned nor discussed. When Judaism declines, for one reason or another, the dietary laws are the first to be assailed, scrutinized, and subsequently abandoned.

Orthodox Jews observe the laws of Kashruth very

rigidly and guard them zealously, for to the orthodox Jew the dietary laws constitute the cornerstone of Judaism and are the most tangible factor in the perpetuation of Jewish life. Conservative Jews, advocating adherence to traditional Judaism, also observe the dietary laws, but they allow some slight modifications and are often lenient when eating outside of the home. Reform Jews, objecting to Jewish legalism on principle, have rejected the dietary laws in their entirety, though many Reform leaders personally adhere to the general code of Kashruth.

No definite reason can be given for the existence, or observance, of the Jewish dietary laws. It has often been stated that the dietary laws are primarily health laws, a contention based upon the longevity of the Jewish people and upon the fact that the Jews were often immune to epidemics which ravaged their Christian neighbors. However, the health theory cannot be stressed in our modern days. A Jewish woman once said to me, "Rabbi, all Jewish dietary regulations are principally health laws, aren't they? Well, Matzos do not agree with me, so I'm eating bread on Passover." To which I replied, "Madam, regardless of your health, loyal Jews do not eat bread on Passover." Another person addressed me as follows: "Moses forbade the use of pork products because they frequently contained the germs that cause trichinosis, but through modern methods pork products are cured and made perfectly safe for food." My terse reply was, "But self-conscious Jews still do not eat pork products." History bears witness to the fact that religious laws, traditionally observed for centuries, cannot always be rationalized. The Bible does not say "Ye shall be healthy," but "Ye shall be holy."

Part Three

THE ETHICS OF JUDAISM

OUR DUTIES TO OUR FELLOW MEN

The third part of Judaism consists of a series of laws which prescribe the daily conduct of the Jew and his relations with his fellow men. These moral concepts of Judaism, as advocated in the Torah and emphasized by the prophets, constitute a Code of Ethics for religious living. The admonitions to practice honesty, justice, truth, righteousness, virtue, love, mercy, and peace are intended to regulate our conduct in life and to formulate our attitudes toward the people with whom we come in daily contact.

The biblical command, "Love thy neighbor as thyself" (Lev. 19:18) is the basis of our moral law and the fundamental principle of the ethics of Judaism. The Christian interpretation of our Golden Rule (love thy neighbor as thyself) is in positive terms, "Do unto others as thou wouldst have others do unto thee." The Jewish interpretation, according to Hillel, is in the negative sense, "Do not unto others what is displeasing to thee." Judaism has accepted both interpretations, though the negative interpretation, restraining man from doing injury or injustice to his fellow man, is more practical in all its implications.

The ethics of Judaism may be divided into four parts (1) Humane Ethics, charitable acts by which man may give his substance, time, and energy to the welfare and happiness of others; (2) Social Ethics, announced with the negative, "Thou shalt not," a series of moral laws which restrain man from doing things that might be detrimental to the welfare and happiness of others; (3) Family Ethics, laws regulating our attitudes and responsibilities to our relatives; (4) Universal Ethics, a series of laws and traditions which describe the obligations which the Jew owes to the country in which he resides, to his community, to his people, to his ancient homeland, and to humanity in general.

1. HUMANE ETHICS

A. Direct Acts of Charity in Helping the Poor

Lincoln said, "God apparently loves the poor people, He made so many of them." There always have been, and there always will be, poor people in the world, and it is our religious duty to help them in every way possible. The ethical laws of Judaism tell us that charity should be given cheerfully, discreetly, and with a full realization that we are all children of God and that it is our sacred duty to help one another. The Hebrew word for charity, "Tz'dokoh" (justice), indicates that the poor person has a right to live as a matter of justice.

As descendants of Abraham, we are also urged to extend hospitality to the stranger. "Love ye the stranger, for ye were once strangers in the land of Egypt" (Deut. 10:19). We are also commanded in the Bible to help the widow and the orphan whenever they become objects of charity. We are especially admonished to relieve human suffering by aiding the sick and the feeble, and by providing shelter and food for the aged. "The rich and the poor meet together; the Lord is the Maker of them all" (Prov. 22:2).

B. Service to Humanity Through Character Building

Charity can also be given without personal contact, by helping the agencies working in that field of social service generally known as "character building." Our religion admonishes us not only to teach our children and to provide instruction for the children of the poor, but also to provide institutions for the education of all the children of the community, rich and poor alike. We must support Talmud Torahs and Yeshivahs, so that our children may be prepared to uphold the traditions of Israel and to live godly, useful lives. We must also maintain, as a religious duty, the many secular institutions that function as character building agencies— schools, colleges, libraries, parks, playgrounds, recreational centers. We must help people in securing employment and in all their economic or domestic adjustments. We must help those who have gone astray to return to the path of virtue and to a useful life. The Hebrew expression, "G'millus Chesed," acts of kindness, covers every type of direct charity which the Jew is admonished to practice as a part of his religion. In the "Ethics of the Fathers" one of our sages states that "G'millus Chesed" is one of the foundations upon which the world rests.

In addition to acts of direct charity, as enumerated above, the Ethics of Judaism emphasize the importance of personal service or indirect charity that may be given to rich and poor alike. The Jew is told to give not only of his substance, but also of himself and of his personality, for the welfare and happiness of others. The following is a partial list of *indirect charities* that are universally practiced in Jewish life:

C. VISITING THE SICK

"Bikkur cholim," or visiting the sick, is one of the earliest religious acts practiced by the Jewish people and is considered to be a great *Mitzvah*. It is one of the noble deeds for which, according to the Mishnah, "one receives but a slight recompense (the fruit) in this world and the main reward in the world to come" (Peah Ch. 1). It is an act of personal kindness through which one gives of himself for the happiness of others. One of the sages of the Talmud states that "one who visits the sick takes away a sixtieth part of his friend's illness" (Nedarim 39). The Talmud further remarks that "he who visits the sick practices one of the noble virtues that are attributed to God" (Sotah 114).

D. Last Rites to the Dead

One of the most important acts of personal service is ministering to the dead. The rabbis tell us that every service given to the dead is an act of "true kindness" (Chessed shell Emmes), because we do not anticipate anything in return. Those people who take care of the preparation and burial of the dead are known in Israel as the *Chevrah Kadisha,* the "holy society." When we cannot participate in the preparation of the body or in its burial, we are to pay our respects to the dead by attending the funeral. "Tz'dokoh Tatzil Mimovess" (Prov. 10:2) "Acts of kindness take away the sting of death."

E. Comforting the Mourners

During the week of *Shivah* (the seven days of mourning), we are to visit mourners and express our condolences to them. We are to sympathize with them in their bereavement and, through words of comfort, assure them that they are not alone in this world. While this type of indirect charity is universal in character, it assumes a religious aspect when, in conformity with Jewish tradition, we say to the mourners, "May God comfort you and all those who mourn the loss of Zion and Jerusalem."

F. Peace Making

"Israel's mission is peace," and it is also the mission of every Israelite to "seek peace and pursue it." When nations quarrel, war results; when individuals fight, suffering and misery come to those involved. It is the duty of the Jew to bring peace to people who are in disagreement. Even though the peacemaker is seldom, if ever, rewarded for his efforts, he finds his reward in the fact that he has made unhappy people happy. This personal service is an indirect charity which, like visiting the sick, may be given to rich and poor alike. "The world rests upon three foundations: truth, justice, and peace" (Ethics of the Fathers 1:18).

G. Thinking Charitably of Others

Every human being is a composite creature of good and evil, with some evil in even the most virtuous person, and some good in the most wicked. It is possible to point to a man's virtues and speak of him with praise, or to emphasize his evil traits and speak of him in derogatory terms.

It is easy to condemn one's neighbor and pass judgment upon him, but before doing this the Jew should ask himself, "What would I have done if I were driven by the same urge or lured by the same temptations?" In the Ethics of the Fathers, Hillel warns us, "Do not judge your neighbor until you have been in his place" (Ch. 2:6). We must appraise our fellow men with kindness, with a sense of fairness, and with genuine good-will. "To judge your neighbor properly, place him on the scale of merit" (Pirke Aboth, Ch. 1:5).

H. Contributing to the Happiness of Others

The Humane Ethics of Judaism further tell us that there are many things that one can and should do to bring joy and comfort to others. Such small things as a pleasant word, a deserved compliment, a kindly smile, a cheerful letter, a timely gift, etc., can bring encouragement and happiness. With these we perform acts of indirect charity even though we ourselves may not always be aware of it.

KINDNESS TO ANIMALS

Judaism also commands us to be kind to animals. In our Code of Laws (Shulchan Aruch) there is a special chapter on *Tzaar Baalei Chayim*, "How to avoid causing pain to living beings," in which we are told to treat animals and birds humanely as well as to give sympathy and kindness to all living beings.

2. SOCIAL ETHICS

In this chapter of the Ethics of Judaism, "Social Ethics," are contained the biblical and Talmudic rules based on a series of negative laws beginning with the words, "Thou shalt not!" The ethical slogan, "Love thy neighbor as thyself," was interpreted negatively by Hillel in the words, "Do not unto thy neighbor what is displeasing to thee," and our Torah contains a great many negative commandments, all intended to prevent us from doing harm to others. We are not to misappropriate, nor destroy, nor injure anything which belongs to our fellow men, as outlined in the following paragraphs.

A. LIFE AND HEALTH

Man, created in the image of God, is the crown of creation; his life is a sacred trust to be cherished and protected. One of God's first commandments to man was an order to the sons of Noah to refrain from shedding human blood. The Talmud goes to the extent of saying that each individual is a little world by himself, and therefore "He who destroys a human life is as if he had destroyed a world, and he who saves a human life is as if he had saved a world" (Sanhedrin 37). Ethical Judaism places great value upon human life and upon the dignity of human personality; it is unalterably opposed to any ideology which minimizes the value of human life.

The sixth of the ten commandments, "Thou shalt not kill," does not only restrain us from destroying life, but also forbids us to harm anyone physically. Because a healthy body and a healthy mind are essential to the enjoyment of life, and every injury to man, physical or mental, impairs his life, we are commanded not to do anything that might injure the life or well being of ourselves or others.

The Torah sanctions capital punishment as a safeguard of society—"He who sheds man's blood, his blood shall be shed by man" (Gen. 9:6). However, even in ancient Palestine where Jewish laws were rigorously adhered to, attempts were made to avoid inflicting the supreme penalty upon sinners. The Talmud even goes to the extent of saying that "A Sanhedrin which ordered the execution of a murderer once in seven years was considered to be a cruel court of justice"(Makkoth 7). Today, many modern sociologists, prompted by humanitarian motives, oppose capital punishment and try to influence State legislatures to eliminate it, and Jewish groups, Orthodox and Reform, have gone on record as opposed to capital punishment. But even though capital punishment is a controversial issue, the command, "Thou shalt not kill" is, and will continue to be, one of the fundamental principles of Judaism. The only exception sanctioned by Judaism is the unavoidable killing of human beings in the pursuit of a just war.

Judaism also contains rules of personal ethics which state man's duties to himself. Man is composed of two parts, body and soul, both of which must be protected if he is to enjoy life. Those negative laws which prohibit him from doing injury to the body of others also restrict him from doing harm to himself. Suicide is as serious a sin as murder because it actually destroys a human life. And while Judaism frowns upon excessive physical indulgences, it also looks with disfavor upon self-inflicted pain or discomfort. According to the Talmud, "He who refrains from food without cause is considered a sinner" (Taanith 11).

Man must preserve and cherish his soul, the basic element of his life. In order to keep his soul clean and holy, the Jew is admonished to cultivate clean thoughts and to devote his leisure hours to the ennobling study of the Torah. He is also admonished, in a series of rules, to care for the health and cleanliness of his body.

B. Man and His Possessions

Every human being has possessions which he calls his own, and no one has the right to deprive him of them. Even a baby points at its garments, or toys, and speaks of them as "mine," and every human being possesses something, be it much or little. The ethical laws of Judaism tell us not to take away, or destroy, anything belonging to another person; they even forbid us to "desire" anything which belongs to others. The tenth commandment, "Lo Tachmod" ("Thou shalt not covet anything that belongs to thy neighbor"), is the only one of the ten commandments that is given twice, both in Exodus and in Deuteronomy, in order to emphasize its importance in our ethical relations with our fellow men. In the Ethics of the Fathers we are told, "Be as considerate of the property of your neighbor as you are of your own." The most direct law safeguarding man's possessions is the eighth commandment, "Thou shalt not steal."

C. Humans as Property

Judaism has always been, and always will be, opposed to slavery and to the possession of human beings as personal property. Yet there are times when an individual may speak of a human being as "mine." Take, for instance, the seventh commandment, "Thou shalt not commit adultery," universally recognized as one of the cornerstones of civilization, as a safeguard of the home which is the foundation of society. This negative law is based primarily on the principle of "possession," for the man who points to a woman and speaks of her as "my" wife has a moral right to claim her, physically and mentally, as his own. The same is true of the woman who points to a man as "my" husband. Love and affection are abstract sentiments, but they are powerful factors in domestic life, determining unique laws of possession.

We may cite another case to illustrate this point. A rich man may take a poor child and offer it a good home, a good education, and an excellent future, but if that child was taken without the consent of its parents, it was, actually, kidnaped. The child belongs to its parents who speak of it as "ours," and though the rich man in question may have the best of motives, he has no right to take the child from the people to whom it rightfully "belongs." The principle of possession thus includes the possession of persons, and the admonition "Thou shalt not steal" may be applied to human affections and to human beings as well as to personal property.

D. The Use of Wealth

The possession of wealth is usually denoted by the collective word "Capital." Religion protects a man's right to his capital and to all the things which constitute his lawful possessions. It has been claimed that organized religion, of the synagogue or of the church, either favors the rich or is actually controlled by them. This may be true in certain instances, but is not true as a general principle.

Judaism has a great many restrictive laws against capital, and when capital is engaged in money lending, it has many prohibitions to comply with. "Lo Tachbol," "Do not take bed clothes, or warm garments, as a pledge." Also, "Lo Tashich," "Do not take interest when lending money to a fellow Jew." The practice of "G'millus Chessed," lending money to each other without interest, is one of the best examples of ethical Judaism in practice. In Psalm 15 we are given a list of persons who will ascend "God's holy mountain," and one of them is "He who does not lend his money on usury."

The biblical law allowing the Jew to take interest from the non-Jew may be due to the fact that in biblical times the gap between Jew and pagan was so wide that when the Jew lent money to the non-Jew, he could not possibly consider it as an act of "G'millus Chessed"; it was a purely business transaction. The same principle applied to the non-Jew lending money to the Jew. In the Middle Ages the Jew was actually forced into the practice of money lending. He was forbidden by the law of the State to own real estate, his wealth was therefore in cash money, and that became his stock in trade. Secondly, the church frequently issued decrees prohibiting the trade of money lending to Christians and forcing it upon the Jews.

E. Employer and Employee

Ethical Judaism constantly warns the employer to deal fairly with the laborer and to heed the law of "Lo Tonu," "Do not cheat." Another restrictive measure against the employer is contained in the words "Lo Tirdeh," "Do not drive him rigorously to do his labors." Still another admonition is "Lo Tolin," "Do not allow the wages of the hired man to stay with you overnight." The Talmud has a ruling that "a laborer may quit in the midst of his work, but the employer cannot discharge the laborer in the middle of the day" (Babba Metzia 83).

Judaism safeguards and protects the interests of labor, but it also restrains it by many negative laws. The admonition "Lo Tonu," "Do not cheat," applies not only to the employer, but also to the laborer who must safeguard his employer's interests. The laborer is justified in demanding a wage commensurate with his work, but he must not expect more than is due him. He must neither diminish nor destroy the possessions of his employer, nor waste the time for which he is being paid; he must work faithfully and loyally.

F. Justice to Humanity

The performance of justice is usually presented in positive terms, such as "do justice" or "justice, justice shalt thou pursue." Actually, however, justice is not performed in a positive manner; it is achieved by obeying negative laws, such as "Do not cheat," "Do not bear false witness against thy neighbor," "Do not rob your neighbor of his rights," "Do not abuse the poor nor oppress the weak." It is through strict adherence to these negative laws that we perform the ideals of justice as advocated in the Torah and by the prophets.

G. Human Rights

Ethical Judaism also admonishes us not to deprive a man of his rights, a possession frequently more valuable than material goods. In addition to physical existence, most of the people of the world cherish the enjoyment of freedom, the most fundamental of human rights. Of course, human rights are not uniform and cannot be described in definite terms. They vary in different localities and with the different positions of individuals. For instance, an invalid is entitled to food, shelter, and comfort, while a healthy individual is entitled to opportunities for growth, power, and self expression. Then again, there are many people endowed by nature with technical or mental abilities who are entitled to the right of turning these abilities into productive or lucrative channels. These are potential rights which should not be suppressed or unfairly exploited. Human rights of every kind, whether statutory or potential, constitute one's personal possessions. They are rigidly protected by the laws of ethical Judaism.

H. Honor and Reputation

In addition to life and material possessions, every person possesses his "honor," an intangible asset made up of his name, reputation, and standing in the community. The social ethics of Judaism, employing the negative, "Thou shalt not," admonish us not to do or say anything that might hurt a person's reputation. We are constantly warned to safeguard human personality and to help the individual retain his honor and reputation.

"The honor of your neighbor shall be as dear to you as your own honor" (Abboth 2:10). God created man in His own image; He made him "but little lower than the angels and crowned him with honor and glory" (Ps. 8:6). To maintain that honor and glory is the task of every human being. Judaism tells us that "putting a man to shame" is as serious a crime as the "shedding of man's blood." The admonition, "Do not insult anyone," runs through the pages of the Talmud. One of the sages of the Talmud even goes to the extent of saying that "a man should rather throw himself into a fiery furnace than insult his neighbor in public" (Babba Metzia 59a).

I. The Evil of Falsehood

"Thou shalt not bear false witness against thy neighbor." The ninth of the ten commandments warns us not to bring suffering or unhappiness to others through false accusations. Telling a lie is in itself a religious misdemeanor, but telling a lie with the intention of doing harm to a man's honor is an ethical sin of serious proportions. Through falsehoods human lives have been impaired or completely destroyed, and through false accusations many a person has lost his possessions, his freedom, and his honor. Judaism therefore warns us to refrain from every malicious falsehood. "Ye shall not steal, nor deal falsely, nor lie one to another" (Lev. 19:11). The Psalmist describes the man of ethical perfection in these words: "Who shall ascend the hill of the Lord, and who shall dwell in His holy place? He who hath clean hands and a pure heart, who hath not lifted up his soul unto falsehood, nor sworn deceitfully" (Ps. 24).

J. The Sin of Slander

"Thou shalt not go up and down slandering people" (Lev. 19:16). Judaism severely denounces the "evil
tongue" which slanders people, it considers spreading
evil reports and malicious defamation of character as
ugly sins. The prophets repeatedly spoke of calumny—
Loshon Horoh—as the evil of a corrupt society. The
Psalms and Proverbs abound with denunciations of
those who spread calumny, and the Talmud constantly
warns us to avoid the evils of slander and idle gossip.
One of the sages of the Talmud states that while all sinners are forgiven on Yom Kippur, the slanderer is not
forgiven until he has made satisfactory apologies to the
person slandered. A "Takanah" (religious decree) from
the period of the Gaonim punishes the slanderer with
excommunication.

The Midrash tells us that the majority of the Israelites
who left Egypt under Moses were not allowed to enter
the Promised Land because they produced the ten spies
who brought in slanderous reports about the country.
It further explains why Miriam, after slandering her
brother Moses, was stricken with leprosy. Her punishment was an indication that the slanderer, like the leper,
is a menace to society. The sages of the Talmud were
severe in their utterances against the man who assails
the honor of his fellow man. "Four classes will be ex-
cluded from the Divine Presence: scoffers, liars, hypo-
crites, slanderers" (Sotah 42). The Talmud speaks of the
slanderous tongue as "telitai," a "three-fold sinner": it
ruins the slanderer, the listener, and the maligned
(Babba Batra 165a). Jewish law not only forbids us to
utter evil reports, but also to listen to them. "Thou shalt

not take up a false report" (Exodus 23:1), and "He who giveth ear to a mischievous tongue encourages lies" (Prov. 17:4). The Jew therefore prays, at the conclusion of the "Amidah," "Oh God, guard my tongue from evil, and my lips from speaking guile."

3. FAMILY ETHICS

Judaism has a series of family ethics which regulate our relations with the people who are near and dear to us, who are our own, and with whom we come in daily contact. These ethical or "moral" duties are contained in the Torah and are repeatedly stressed in the Talmud.

A. PARENT AND CHILD

One of the rabbis of the Talmud makes this unusual statement: "God cannot be with every person, everywhere, at all times, so He created a substitute to take His place—the love of parents." Parents love their children with a religious fervor, a fact which the parents themselves do not always realize. My observations lead me to venture a personal opinion that the further removed a Jewish person is from the synagogue and from traditional Jewish life, the less is his love for his children. It seems to me as if an inherently religious instinct within the Jewish heart causes Jewish parents to make unusual sacrifices for their children.

Psychologists and educators have often expressed their admiration of this self-sacrificing attitude of Jewish parents. Dr. Charles W. Eliot, late president of Harvard University, once made this significant statement: "As president of Harvard College, I had many opportunities of comparing the strength of the Jewish family sentiment with the Christian. In forty years I never knew a case in which a Jewish family failed to come to the assistance of a son taken seriously ill at Harvard College; while I witnessed many an instance in which a Christian father and mother came reluctantly or not at all, even when I repeatedly urged their coming."

In the Jewish liturgy God is often implored to show such mercy to Israel "as a father pities his children," and the proverbial expression, "a Jewish mother," has come to mean a woman of great love and tenderness. There are no Jewish laws ordering parents to provide for the physical needs of their children, for such laws were obviously considered unnecessary. There are, however, repeated admonitions to parents to provide for the spiritual needs of their children. "Thou shalt teach them (the words of God) diligently unto thy children," and "Thou shalt tell thy children. . . ." It is the duty of Jewish parents to give their children an education which will prepare them for a moral and religious life.

The duties of children to their parents occupy an important place in the teachings of ethical Judaism. According to the Talmud, each individual is owned by three partners: God, father, and mother (Kiddushin 30). The Jewish child is repeatedly told to fulfill every wish of his parents, to obey every one of their orders, to show them every token of affection, and to make them happy through his good conduct.

The fifth commandment, "Honor thy father and thy mother," is a fundamental principle in Jewish life, for if the Jew is to practice justice and mercy to others, he must, first of all, be respectful and kind to his own parents. The Shulchan Aruch, under the heading "Kibbud Av V'aim" (How to honor father and mother), gives a series of laws which are to be followed by the Jew in the performance of the fifth commandment. There we are expressly told that we are in duty bound to recognize the wisdom, the experience, and the services of our parents; we are to honor them, to help them, and to do everything in our power to contribute to their comfort and happiness. We are to support and protect them when they become old, weak, or poor; and when they are departed from this life, we are to honor their name and memory, and hold in respect the wishes they expressed when alive.

B. HUSBAND AND WIFE

The marriage vow unites man and wife in holy matrimony and they become, according to the Bible, "as one flesh." Judaism regulates the marital relations between husband and wife and prohibits infidelity with the seventh commandment, "Thou shalt not commit adultery." Every infringement on the marriage vow and every act of infidelity, physical or mental, are severely denounced. Many books of the Talmud, dealing with the laws of matrimony, set forth the duties which husband and wife must perform in order to maintain the sanctity of the Jewish home. In stressing the need of mutual understanding and cooperation between husband and wife, the Talmud has a quaint saying: "When the wife is of low stature, physically or mentally, the husband should stoop down to her level" (Babba Meziah 59). Love and devotion between husband and wife have made the Jewish home through the ages a sanctuary in miniature. "When husband and wife live a meritorious life, the *Shechinah* (God's presence) is in their midst" (Sotah 17).

C. RELATIVES

Judaism also calls for harmony and mutual assistance among all the members of a family. Brothers and sisters are to cultivate a spirit of true love for each other. When, in the absence of parents, the oldest brother (or sister) assumes the role of the parents, he is to be given the respect due him in accordance with the biblical law of "Birthright."

When one member of a family is successful, all the members should rejoice with him and share in his happiness. On the other hand, when one member of a family is in distress, all the other members should come to his rescue. The prophet Isaiah, in his famous sermon on ethics, urges us to support poor relatives when he says, "Do not stay aloof from thine own flesh" (Is. 58:7).

There are Jewish laws forbidding marriages between kinfolk (Lev. 18), and there are also laws granting the rights of inheritance to relatives in the absence of children (Numb. 27), but there are no specific laws regulating our attitude towards our relatives. Nevertheless, we must act in conformity with an accepted tradition in Israel by showing love and affection to all the members of our families. Adherence to this tradition is shown by the generous support American Jews are giving today to members of their families abroad.

4. UNIVERSAL ETHICS

Ethical Judaism aims to improve the individual so that he will be of service to society as a whole. From time immemorial, people have organized themselves into tribes, groups, and nations, and we are asked to further the interests of all organized activities. The Jewish people have been repeatedly told that the scope of Judaism is not limited to ethical concepts which concern individuals, but includes a series of universal ethics for the improvement of the world and for the happiness of the entire human race.

A. Patriotism

In the life of a nation the individual is part of a greater whole. The nation nourishes and protects the citizen, but demands loyalty, sacrifice, and service in return. Every act against the government, even though it may be within the framework of legality, is an ethical misdemeanor. Our religion maintains that in order to be a good, religious man one must first be a good citizen, for obedience to the law of the land supersedes obedience to the law of religion. In every synagogue prayers have always been recited for the welfare of the nation and of its ruler. Our people who have lived in many lands, have always been loyal citizens, or subjects, in all these lands because they followed the mandate of Judaism which insists upon patriotic loyalty as the ethical duty of every Jew. The Talmud repeatedly says *Dino D'malchusso Dino*, "the law of the land is the Law."

B. The Jewish Community

Every Jewish person has obligations to the Jewish community of which he is a part and around which his social and religious life evolves. "Separate not thyself from the community" (Pirke Aboth 2:5) is sound advice to every Jew. History indicates that through the centuries our people have disliked living in rural sections and have preferred living in cities. The reasons for such preferences are obvious. The city, with its larger Jewish population, made it possible for the Jew to participate in public worship, to secure the necessary *Minyan* for reciting the Kaddish during the period of mourning and at Yahrzeits, to obtain teachers for the religious education of his children, to secure kosher food, to establish and maintain social intercourse with his co-religionists. These reasons, once of paramount importance, still influence Jewish life to a large extent, for even the modern Jew dislikes living as an isolated individual and prefers to be part of a community.

It is an ethical obligation upon every Jew to belong to a synagogue. From birth to burial there are many occasions, such as Bris Milahs, Barmitzvahs, weddings, funerals, etc., on which the Jew needs the synagogue and its official representatives. In addition to synagogues, every community has its organized activities, and some of the larger cities maintain charitable, social, and educational institutions. It is the duty of every Jew to support, in proportion to his means, every organization or institution whose activities contribute to the welfare of the Jewish community or to the credit of the Jewish people.

C. Universal Israel

Another of our ethical duties is to serve the Jewish people of the world. "All Jews are responsible for each other" is a Talmudic maxim often quoted by both friend and foe, for every Jew, wherever he may live, belongs to that great fraternity known as *K'lal Yisroel*—universal Israel. Every Jew is a link in a long chain which encircles the globe.

When evil times come upon the House of Israel, no Jew, however prominent or secure, should stand aloof from his people. As Mordecai said to Esther, "Deem not in thy soul that the resident of the Royal House will escape the fate of all the Jews" (Esther 4:13). Every Jew is "his brother's keeper," and when the Jew in one part of the world suffers, his brethren in other parts of the world must come to his rescue. The invisible, yet indivisible, unity in Israel contributed largely, and will continue to contribute, to the survival of our people.

D. Palestine as a National Homeland

Next to our duties at home and abroad, it is our duty to help restore Palestine as the national home for the Jewish people. For centuries we have prayed, and we are still praying, for the rebuilding of Zion and Jerusalem. Now the Zionist movement has imposed upon us a new task. We are not only to pray, but also to work, for the re-establishment of our homeland.

It is superfluous to discuss the issues of Zionism, for the Zionist movement has ceased to be a subject for discussion and is now an integral part of Jewish life. True enough, there are many Jews who refuse to subscribe to the Zionist program in its entirety, but our history has shown that no movement or ideology created by the Jewish people was ever accepted by all the Jews everywhere, with the sole exception of the theory of the Unity of God as promulgated in the *Sh'ma Yisroel.*

A vast majority of the Jewish people of the world has accepted Zionism and contributed millions of dollars toward the realization of its program. The Jewish people of America are actively participating, in one way or another, in the promotion of the Zionist ideal, and the program of Jewish education in America is almost completely dominated by a spirit of love for Zion. While European and Palestinean Jews may disagree and argue along party lines within Zionism, they are practically unanimous in their opinion as to the potentialities of the Zionist movement for the future of our people. The Jewish children of Eastern European countries, such as Poland, Lithuania, Latvia, etc., speak Hebrew with the Palestinean dialect since they are being prepared, physically and psychologically, to be *Chalutzim* in Palestine.

Zionism is now the most absorbing ideology in the life of the Jewish people, and even those who disagree with its theories admit its positive benefits. In view of the fact that the Zionist movement is now accepted, in one form or another, by the vast majority of the Jewish people, it is the duty of every Jew to support the efforts of this majority. It is therefore proper to state that the universal ethics of Judaism impose upon the modern Jew a moral obligation to help in the restoration of Palestine as the national Jewish homeland.

E. The Brotherhood of Man

Judaism not only persists in the theory of one God, but also teaches the doctrine of one humanity. "Have we not

all one father? Hath not one God created us?" (Malachi
2:10). The Talmud advances the theory that God gathered dust from the four corners of the earth to make
Adam, the father of the human race, thus giving a common origin to all God's children in all parts of the world.
This theory calls for the elimination of racial and religious barriers and for the practice of tolerance and good
will.

The Brotherhood of Man is an ethical theory to which
all religions subscribe. Judaism, the monotheistic religion of civilization, maintains that human progress is
possible only through the spirit of true religion and
through friendly relationships among all the peoples of
the universe. The biblical ideals of peace and mutual
helpfulness are visualized by the prophet Micah who predicts the coming of the day, "When they shall sit every
man under his vine and under his fig tree; and none shall
make them afraid" (Micah 4:4). When the Brotherhood
of Man becomes a reality, the Kingdom of God will be
established on earth.

F. UNIVERSAL PEACE

Judaism maintains that the Messianic Era will bring
peace and happiness to all mankind. Although the universal ethics of every religion advocate the ideal of peace
on earth, Judaism embellishes that ideal by linking it
with the Messianic Age.

The ancient Hebrews fought the battles of Jehovah
and took part in many wars. Nevertheless, in the course
of time, they developed the theory that an ideal state of
human relations is possible only with universal peace.
The rabbis of the Talmud tell us that God will not reign
supreme on earth as long as there are wars between na-

tions. "The sword and the Book of God came to the world simultaneously, but they cannot exist together; when the sword rages, the Book of God is rejected" (Sifri, Ekev.).

It has been stated that the ideal of the ancient Greeks was "Beauty," that the goal of the Romans was "Power," but the slogan of the Hebrews was "Peace." Throughout the centuries the Jewish people have greeted each other with the word, "Shalom"—peace. According to George Foote Moore: "The Hebrew *shalom* has a wider meaning than the English 'peace.' For the individual it is a welfare of every kind, sound health, prosperity, security, contentment, and the like. In the relations of men to their fellows it is the harmony without which the welfare of the individual or the community is impossible."

National welfare and prosperity are not only incomplete, but inconceivable, without peace. Judaism which seeks the well-being of individuals and of nations, speaks in glowing terms of the blessing of peace among men. It hopes and prays for the fulfillment of the prophecy of Isaiah when, in the end of days, "they shall beat their swords into plowshares, and their spears into pruning-hooks; nation shall not lift up sword against nation, neither shall they learn war any more" (Isaiah 2:2–4).

SUMMARY

Ethical conduct, or morality, is the sanctification of human behavior. Judaism, especially in its prophetic interpretation, distinguishes between ethical holiness and ritual holiness, asserting that ethical holiness often excels the holiness of ceremonial practices. However, it is wrong to describe ritual holiness as religion and ethical holiness as mere humanism, for while Judaism sanctifies every ritual act performed in honor of God, it also emphasizes the importance of every ethical deed performed for the welfare of man. Ethics and religion are indissolubly bound together in Judaism.

PART FOUR

CUSTOMS AND SYMBOLS OF JUDAISM

CUSTOMS AND SYMBOLS OF JUDAISM

In the second part of this book are described the sacred laws of Judaism as they are observed in the synagogue, in the home, and in connection with the observance of holidays. The material given there does not include the diverse customs and symbols which form the background of Jewish life and make it different from the way of life of other people. In the following pages are presented, in concise form and with brief explanations, many of the customs and symbols of Judaism.

Jewish customs vary in character and in importance. Some of them are "Mideoraisso," practiced in conformity with divine commands as recorded in the Torah; others are "Midrabbonon," rabbinical precepts that were laid down in the days of the Talmud; still others are "Takonos," decrees issued in various periods of Jewish history by rabbinical authorities. Some of the customs are "Dinnim," religious laws that are universally observed; others are "Minhaggim," accepted practices of local importance; still others exist because they were suggested by biblical quotations.

Symbols are, as a general rule, the external expression and the means of identification of organized groups—national, social, and religious. Organized religion has many symbols, and Judaism is no exception. It is true that Judaism forbids making and worshiping idols and images, but it does not prohibit making objects intended either to adorn the sanctuary or to symbolize religious practices. Some of these symbols originated in biblical days;

others date back to the days of the Talmud; still others were adopted in the Middle Ages. Symbols occupy a position of importance in the synagogue, in the home, and, to some extent, in every walk of Jewish life. The customs and symbols of Judaism are classified in the following eight chapters:

1. CUSTOMS AND PRACTICES IN THE SYNAGOGUE

1. *Minyan.* Ten Jewish males, aged thirteen or over, constitute a quorum, or "Minyan," for conducting a public Service in the synagogue (T'phillah b'tzibur). The origin of this ruling may be found in the Bible where the ten spies who brought in a discouraging report about the promised land were called by God "an evil congregation" (Numb. 14:27).
2. *Turning East.* During the recital of that set of prayers known as "Sh'mono Essrei" or "Amidah," the Jew stands up and turns to the East, symbolic of the rising sun and of Palestine, the historic land of the East.
3. *Reading of the Torah.* The most important ceremony in the synagogue is the reading of the Torah. Jewish men participate in that public Service when they are called up to pronounce a "Brochoh" before and after the reading of the Torah (Aliyoss). A Cohen (a descendant of Aaron) is called first, then a Levite (a descendant of the tribe of Levi, but not of the priestly family), then the Israelites.
4. *Bar Mitzvah.* When a Jewish boy reaches the age of thirteen, he becomes religiously of age. He is called up to pronounce a "Brochoh" over the Torah and is officially accepted as a member of the Jewish community. The term Bar Mitzvah is found in the Talmud (B.M. 96a), and applies to every grown Israelite. In the Ethics of the Fathers (5:24) the age of thirteen is given for religious responsibility.

161

5. *Gomel Benshen,* a special expression of gratitude, is recited by the Jew in the synagogue upon his recovery from a serious illness or upon his escape from a grave emergency.

6. *Duchenen,* the popular name of that ceremony in which the Cohen adjusts his fingers, in a traditional manner, and confers the priestly Benediction upon the people. This is in keeping with God's order to the sons of Aaron, "Thus ye shall bless the children of Israel. . . ." (Numb. 6:23.) A Levite pours water upon the Cohen's hands prior to the ceremony. "Duchenen," or blessing the people, is a part of the synagogue Service. In the Diaspora it is performed only during the holidays, but in modern Palestine it is a daily rite.

7. *Kneeling in Prayer* has been discontinued as a general practice in Judaism. However, it is done in the synagogue on Rosh Hashanah and on Yom Kippur.

8. *Separation of Sexes.* In accordance with an established custom in Israel, the Orthodox synagogue separates men and women during divine Services. Conservative and Reform Temples have discontinued this practice.

9. *Organ Music.* Since the destruction of the Second Temple (in 70 C. E.) the use of organ music has been banned from the synagogue. It was claimed that the synagogue in the lands of exile was not sacred enough to use the same type of instrument as was used at Services in the Temple at Jerusalem. This ruling has become a tradition in Israel. It is rigidly adhered to by the Orthodox synagogue, but all Reform Temples, and many Conservative Temples, disregard the tradition and make use of organ music as a part of their ritual.

2. SYMBOLS AND RELIGIOUS OBJECTS IN THE SYNAGOGUE

1. *Ner Tamid,* the perpetual light. In every synagogue there is a perpetual light, placed either in a vessel containing oil and a wick or in an ornamental receptacle containing an electric bulb. It is usually suspended from the ceiling in front of the Holy Ark. The Ner Tamid had its origin in the early days of Israel's history. A perpetual lamp burned in the sanctuary in the wilderness and also in the Temple at Jerusalem (Lev. 6:6). It was later transferred from the "Greater Temple" in Jerusalem to the synagogue, the "Lesser Temple," in all parts of the world (Mikdash M'at). Lighting the Ner Tamid and placing the scrolls of the Torah in the Holy Ark are the principal ceremonies in the dedication of a synagogue.

2. *Menorah.* The original Menorah, or seven-branched candelabra, was made by Bezalel for the Tabernacle, and a duplicate of it was placed in the Temple at Jerusalem. Its counterpart is to be found in practically every synagogue. Its primary purpose was, and still is, to symbolize the light of the Torah. The Menorah has often been recognized as the symbol of universal Judaism. Many Orthodox Jews, looking with disfavor upon the use of a vessel or instrument that was used in the Temple at Jerusalem (see Organ Music) light only six of the seven branches of the Menorah.

3. *Mogen Dovid* (David's shield), the six pointed star which is supposed to date back to the days of King David, also called Solomon's seal, or Solomon's star. It has no religious significance and even its origin is vague, for it is not mentioned in the Bible nor in the Talmud. However, it is universally displayed and is frequently considered the symbol of the Jewish people.

4. *The Tablets of the Law.* A reproduction of the two tablets of stone, containing the Ten Commandments, is seen in practically every synagogue. It is symbolic of God's Revelation on Mt. Sinai.

5. *Oron Kodesh,* the Holy Ark which contains the scrolls of the Torah. It is a replica of the Ark of the Covenant which was erected in the Tabernacle to house the two tablets of the Ten Commandments and which was subsequently placed in the Holy of Holies in the Temple at Jerusalem. The ornamental drape of the Holy Ark is called "Porochos."

6. *Sefer Torah,* the holy scroll which contains the Pentateuch, or Torah, is the most sacred symbol of Judaism. It is written with indelible ink on parchment which is specially processed for that purpose from calves' skins. The writer, called "Soffer," or "Scribe," is usually a pious man who devotes most of his life to this sacred work.

7. *Kesser Torah,* a figurative crown of the Torah, is usually designed on the "Porochos." This is in keeping with a quotation from the Ethics of the Fathers which lists the crown of the Torah with the crowns of the king and of the High Priest (Ethics 4:17).

8. *The Bimah,* or Almemor, the platform for the reading of the Torah. This pulpit, or reading desk, is

usually decorated with the Mogen Dovid and covered with an embroidered cloth.

9. *Torah Ornaments.* In addition to the ornate embroideries on its cloth mantle, or cover, the Torah is also adorned with many objects of art such as a crown, a breastplate, a pointer, and a pair of "Etz Chayim" (ornaments with bells).

10. *The Lion of Judah* is placed either on the Holy Ark or on the "Porochos." It derives its origin from the time when Jacob, blessing his children before his death, compared Judah to a lion (Gen. 49:9). The Jewish people, descendants of the tribe of Judah, have accepted the lion as their symbol.

11. *Tallis,* the prayer shawl, with the fringes (tzitzis) on each of its four corners. The tzitzis are, according to Moses, to remind the Jew of the commandments of God (Numb. 15:14). The Tallis is worn at the daily morning Services and at the morning Services of the Sabbath and the holidays. The color of the Tallis is usually white, set off by blue or black stripes.

12. *T'phillin,* also called phylacteries, are square boxes containing the biblical chapter of the "Sh'ma" in which we are told, "Thou shalt bind them (the words of God) as a sign upon thy hand, and they shall be for frontlets between thy eyes" (Deut. 6:8). In compliance with that commandment, the T'phillin are put on the upper arm and on the forehead. In addition to the "Sh'ma," the T'phillin contain three other passages of the Bible in which the people of Israel were likewise ordered to put on their persons some objects containing the words of God. Our sages tell us that by placing the T'phillin on the head and on the upper muscle of the arm, we dedicate our

thoughts and our deeds to the service of God (She-
loh). The T'phillin are used at the morning services
on week-days only.

13. *The Siddur* (or T'phillah), the book which contains
a complete arrangement of the prayers used on week-
days, on the Sabbath, and on the holidays.

14. *The Machzor,* the book which contains an arrangement of the prayers recited on the High Holidays
and on the three Festivals.

15. *The Shofar,* the shrill-sounding trumpet made of a
ram's horn. It symbolizes Abraham's obedience on
Mt. Moriah and also God's Revelation on Mt. Sinai.
It is blown after the morning Services in the month
of Ellul, as a part of the Services of Rosh Hashanah,
and at the conclusion of the Neilah Service on Yom
Kippur.

16. *The Kiddush Cup,* an ornamental wine cup that is
used when the Kiddush prayer is recited in the synagogue on the Sabbath and on the festivals.

17. *Spice Box,* used in connection with the Havdalah
prayer on Saturday nights.

18. *Yahrzeit Lights.* In many synagogues special lamps
are lit on Yom Kippur or in connection with the observance of Yahrzeits.

3. SYMBOLS AND PRACTICES IN THE JEWISH HOME

1. *Chanukas Habbayis.* A new home, when occupied by Jewish people, is usually dedicated with a special ceremony called "Chanukas Habbayis" (dedication of the home).
2. *Sanctuary in Miniature.* The Jewish home is often called a sanctuary in miniature because the dietary laws, the Sabbath and holiday ceremonies, and many ethical laws are observed in it.
3. *The Mezuzah* is a piece of parchment on which the two first paragraphs of the "Sh'ma" (Deut. 6:4—Deut. 11:13) are written. The parchment is rolled together, placed in a container, and nailed to the right doorpost of the entrance to the house and to every room. This is done in conformity with the command, "Thou shalt write them on the doorposts of thy house and upon thy gates" (Deut. 6:9).
4. *N'tillas Yodoyim,* washing the hands upon rising in the morning, after touching anything unclean, before offering a prayer, and preceding each meal. It is a religious act performed daily in the Jewish home.
5. *Birchas Hanehenin* is a set of prayers, recited by the observant Jew, before he partakes of either food or drink.
6. *Hamotzi,* the expression of gratitude for bread, is recited before each meal. The word "bread" stands for every type of food.
7. *Benshen,* or "Birchas Hamozon," is a series of pray-

ers that are recited at the conclusion of each meal.

8. *Challah Offering*. When the pious Jewish woman bakes bread, she takes a piece of the dough and throws it in the fire as a "challah offering." This is in keeping with a practice which prevailed in biblical times. After the performance of this religious act, a coin is usually dropped into the charity box.

4. CUSTOMS AND SYMBOLS OF THE SABBATH

1. *Eruv Chatzeros,* uniting of houses into a courtyard. Since it is forbidden to carry articles from one house to another on the Sabbath, a wire is suspended over a group of houses, making them into a community courtyard. Carrying food and other articles is then permitted within this area. This practice is still popular in Europe.

2. *Eruv T'chumin,* combining the boundaries. The Jewish law limits the walking distance on the Sabbath, outside of a city, to a "T'chum," about two miles. When food is deposited on Friday at the terminus, or legal boundary line, the traveler may stop there, eat something, and then walk another "T'chum." This, too, is still practiced in many European towns.

3. *Two Challahs.* Two Sabbath breads (called "Challahs," or "B'roches," or "Barches") are placed on the table, symbolic of the Shewbreads that were displayed in the Tabernacle and changed for each Sabbath.

4. *Covering the Challahs.* We cover the Challahs in order to distinguish them from the original Shewbreads in the Tabernacle that were uncovered.

5. *Blessing the Children.* It is customary, in many countries, for the father of the house to bless his children on Friday night prior to the Kiddush prayer.

6. *Eating of Fish on the Sabbath.* We eat fish on the

Sabbath because fish is the symbol of fertility. When Jacob blessed his grandchildren, he said, "May they multiply like fish in the midst of the land" (Gen. 48:16).

7. *Sholosh S'uddos.* To make the Sabbath complete, three meals are to be eaten on that day. The third meal, late Saturday afternoon, is called "Sholosh S'uddos" and is usually an occasion for singing and religious enthusiasm.

8. *M'laveh Malkah.* This is a special feast, held on Saturday night, to bid farewell to the departing queen, the Sabbath.

(See Chapter on "Sabbath")

5. RELIGIOUS PRACTICES IN JEWISH LIFE

1. *"Bris" or circumcision,* performed on the male child eight days after his birth. This is the oldest religious practice of the Jewish people, for it dates back to the days of the patriarchs and to the covenant (Bris) that was made between God and Abraham. The man who performs the circumcision is called "Mohel." The ceremony is usually performed in the morning. This is done to follow the example of Abraham of whom we are told, "And Abraham arose in the morning."

2. *Pidyon Habben,* the redemption of the first son. A Jewish boy who is his mother's first-born is redeemed when he reaches his thirty-first day. When God smote the first-born of the Egyptians and spared those of the Israelites, He appropriated to Himself the first-born male Israelites, and then gave them as a gift to the Cohen. The "Pidyon Habben" is the ceremony in which the father redeems his child from the Cohen.

3. *Covering the Head.* The observant Jew keeps his head covered while in the synagogue and when offering prayers to God. This is in keeping with an oriental custom requiring people to cover their heads (or faces) when praying to God and when in the presence of a great dignitary. Many Jewish people who have accepted the ways of Western culture still retain this Eastern tradition. It may also be mentioned that many of the Jewish married women in Eastern European countries wear wigs to cover their hair.

4. *Tzitzis.* In addition to the "Tallis" which is worn at Services, the observant male Jew also wears a four-cornered garment, with fringes (Tzitzis) attached to each corner. The garment is called "Arba Kanfos" or "Tallis Koton." The tzitzis are, according to Moses, to remind us of the commandments of God (Numb. 15:40).

5. *Shaatnez.* The Mosaic laws prohibit any kind of "mixture" or hybrid. The observant Jew refrains from wearing "Shaatnez," a garment made of a "mixture" of wool and linen (Deut. 22:11).

6. *Kiddush L'vonoh.* Once a month, during the period of the full moon, pious Jews assemble in the open and, under the moonlight, offer a special prayer of welcome to the moon.

7. *Shinui Hashem,* change of name. When a person is critically ill, a special prayer is offered for his life and his name is changed. This is done by strictly orthodox Jews in accordance with a statement in the Talmud (Rosh Hashanah 16:B): "The decree which seals a man's fate may be annulled by four things: alms, prayer, change of name, change of deeds." The theory is that a patient, decreed to die, is given a new name; he becomes a new person and the decree is annulled.

6. MARRIAGE

1. *The Groom is Called up to the Torah.* On the Sabbath preceding his marriage, the groom is called up to pronounce a benediction over the Torah. This is symbolic of Israel's acceptance of the Torah and of the allegorical wedding between God (the groom) and Israel (the bride).

2. *Marriage in Afternoon or Evening.* Jewish marriages are usually performed either in the afternoon or in the evening. The reason for this is that the first Jewish marriage recorded in the Bible, Isaac's marriage to Rebecca, took place in a field late in the afternoon ("toward evening") (Gen. 24:63).

3. *Bride and Groom Fast on their Wedding Day.* Like Yom Kippur, the wedding day forgives all errors, or sins, that were committed by the groom or bride before their marriage. They therefore observe their wedding day in the same manner as the Jew observes Yom Kippur—by fasting.

4. *The K'subah,* or marriage certificate, is the legal document of the two contracting parties, signed by two witnesses. Jewish marriages are not performed on the Sabbath or on holidays because no legal transactions are entered into on those days.

5. *The Kinyan Sudar* is an oriental affirmation of a contract. This act is performed when the rabbi and the groom hold the same garment, or handkerchief, and the groom agrees to the terms of the K'subah.

6. *Bride Not Seen on Wedding Day.* The groom is not to see the bride before their marriage, so that he will appreciate her more when he does see her.

7. *The Groom Covers the Bride's Face.* This is done, first of all, as a symbol of chastity. It also indicates that the face of the bride shall henceforth be open to the groom but, symbolically, covered to the outside world. It further reminds the bride of Rebecca, the kindly maiden of the Bible, who covered her face when she saw her groom (Isaac) approaching.

8. *The Chuppah,* or canopy under which Jewish couples are married, symbolizes the protection which the groom promises to his bride and the home which the couple is to establish in Israel. The Chuppah further reminds us of the mountain (Sinai) under which our people stood when they were wedded to God.

9. *Man First.* The man goes first to the marriage ceremony because the man was first in the process of creation.

10. *The Bride Is Led to the Chuppah.* The bride is led by her parents or friends (Unterfihrer), as God Himself led the first bride (Eve) to her marriage, "And He brought her unto Adam."

11. *K'dushin,* act of holiness. The marriage ceremony is called K'dushin (Holiness) because the groom says to the bride, "Be thou holy unto me."

12. *The Bride Walks Around the Groom.* This is in keeping with the quotation in the book of Jeremiah (31:21), "The woman encircles the man." It also indicates that henceforth the man is to be fenced around by the woman.

13. *Use of Wine.* Wine is used at the marriage ceremony

because wine "brings joy to God and to man" (Judges 9:13), and marriage is a happy occasion.

14. *The Marriage Ring.* The marriage ring is placed on the index finger of the bride's right hand, the most important of the ten fingers.

15. *Breaking of Glass.* The groom breaks a glass at the conclusion of the ceremony to remind us, during our joy, of the destruction of the Temple at Jerusalem.

16. *Mazel Tov.* "Mazel" is a star or a heavenly symbol, "Tov" means "good." The exclamation "Mazel Tov" after a marriage ceremony expresses a wish that the couple may start life under the guidance of a good, or lucky, star.

17. *Rice Thrown on Couple.* Rice kernels grow in profusion. They are therefore thrown on the bride and groom with the wish, "May you multiply abundantly."

18. *Marriage Restrictions.* Orthodox tradition forbids marriages in the "S'phira" period, between Passover and Shavuos, and also in the period of the "three weeks," from the seventeenth of Tammuz till after the ninth of Ab.

7. DIVORCE, AGUNAH, CHALITZAH

1. *Gett* is the name by which Jewish divorce is known. In America the Gett is performed by Orthodox rabbis only. Conservative rabbis do not, as a rule, issue a Gett, and Reform rabbis neither require nor issue one.

2. *Gett and Legal Divorce.* A Jewish Gett does not constitute a legal separation for the two parties, for the Gett has no legal status in the American courts. An official divorce, issued by a court of justice, is usually secured prior to the Gett.

3. *The Man Gives the Gett to the Woman.* According to Jewish law, the man "takes unto himself a wife," and the man can send her away by means of a bill of divorcement. In accordance with that law, the woman cannot divorce her husband.

4. *Remarriage.* A divorced woman, or a widow, must not remarry for a period of ninety days in order to establish the paternity of a possible child. A divorced woman may remarry her husband if she has not, since her divorce, been married to another man.

5. *Divorce and Cohen.* A member of the priestly tribe, a Cohen, is not allowed to marry a divorced woman.

6. *Agunah,* an abandoned woman. "Agunah" is the name given in Orthodox Jewry to a woman who has been deserted by her husband or whose husband is lost or missing. She is not a widow because her husband's death cannot be ascertained, nor can she secure a divorce because her husband is not present to

give her a Gett. She is just an "Agunah," an abandoned woman who cannot marry again. Many attempts have been made to change this law and to
remedy the status of the "Agunah," but so far without success.

7. *Chalitzah,* a released woman. A childless widow is
required, by Orthodox Jewish law, to get a release
from the brother of her late husband if she desires
to marry again. The ceremony of the release, called
"Chalitzah," is performed by a rabbi in the presence
of witnesses. This is an established practice in Judaism since biblical times, but it is not rigidly adhered
to in modern Jewish life.

8. DEATH AND MOURNING

1. *Tachrichim* (Shrouds). Orthodox Jewish law requires that the dead, rich or poor, be buried in white shrouds. The plain, white shrouds symbolize both purity and the idea of equality in death.
2. *K'riah.* Cutting and tearing garments as a symbol of sorrow is a custom which dates back to biblical days. After tearing his garments, the mourner utters the benediction, "Boruch dayan emmess," "Blessed be He, the righteous Judge."
3. *Covering the Mirrors* in a house of sorrow symbolizes a desire on our part to suppress vanity in a time of sorrow.
4. *S'uddas Havro'oh.* After the funeral, a family meal is prepared by neighbors or friends. Round articles of food, such as eggs, are eaten as a symbol of the cycle of life.
5. *Shivah,* litterally "seven." Orthodox law, dating back to biblical days, orders that a period of mourning for the dead be observed for seven days (Shivah). During that week the mourners, with shoes (oriental symbol of luxury) removed, sit on low benches to signify their low spirit. The "Shivah" rules are waived on Sabbath and on holidays.
6. *Kaddish,* a traditional prayer for the dead since the days of Rabbi Akiba (Second Century c. e.) is recited during the Shivah week and then continued daily for eleven months.
7. *Comforting the Mourners.* The importance of fol-

lowing the dead to their final resting place, and comforting the mourners in their days of sorrow is repeatedly emphasized in biblical and traditional Judaism.

8. *Yahrzeit,* the anniversary of the death of a parent, or of a near relative, is observed by lighting a Yahrzeit candle that burns for twenty-four hours and by reciting the Kaddish in memory of the dead.

9. *Yizkor Memorial Prayers* are recited in the synagogue on Yom Kippur, on the last day of Passover, on Sh'mini Atzeres, and on the second day of Shavuos.

10. *Visiting the Cemetery.* It is an established custom in Israel to visit the cemetery before and after Rosh Hashanah and to offer prayers at the graves of departed relatives.

11. *Exclusion of the Cohen.* A Cohen retains his ancestral state of priestly holiness by being aloof from death. He is forbidden to handle the dead, to be in the same house with a dead person, and even to enter the cemetery grounds.

PART FIVE

THE SOURCES OF JUDAISM

I. The Bible
II. The Talmud
III. The Codes of Jewish Laws

I. THE BIBLE

The Bible is the first and foremost source of Judaism. It contains the religious laws which the Jewish people have accepted for their guidance. Its name derives from the Greek word "Biblia" (book); it is also called "Holy Writ," or "Kissvei Kodesh"—"Holy Scriptures." Although the Bible was not written by one man nor at one time, we believe that each of its many authors wrote under divine inspiration. The Jewish Bible—the Old Testament—was not intended to serve as a book of religion but as a book of life and, true to life, it depicts human vices as well as human virtues, though it urges the pursuit of the latter for man's welfare and happiness.

According to Jewish tradition (Massorah) the Bible is a collection of twenty-four books, with the Pentateuch, or Torah, considered as one book. Usually, however, the Pentateuch is counted as five books, making the total of the Holy Scriptures twenty-eight books. Sometimes, too, each book of the twelve minor prophets is counted individually and the Holy Writ becomes a collection of thirty-nine books. The Bible is divided into three parts: (1) Torah (Pentateuch), (2) Neviim (Prophets), (3) Chessuvim (Writings). The initial letters of the three portions of the Bible are T. N. Ch., pronounced "TaNaCh."

1. TORAH

The first and most important part of the Bible is the
Pentateuch (a Greek word meaning "five books"), or the
Five Books of Moses, best known as the Torah. It is also
called "Chumesh" (book of five) and is frequently referred to as the "Law" or the "Law of Moses." The books
of the Pentateuch are as follows:

Genesis (B'reshis) contains the stories of creation, of
Adam and Eve, of Noah and the flood, of the three Patriarchs—Abraham, Isaac, and Jacob—, of Joseph, and of
the coming of the Hebrews into Egypt.

Exodus (Sh'mos) opens with an account of the enslave-
ment and suffering of the Hebrews in the land of Egypt
and then tells of the birth of Moses, of the vision at the
burning bush, of the Exodus of the Israelites from Egypt.
It describes the miraculous crossing of the Red Sea, God's
Revelation on Mt. Sinai and the giving of the ten commandments, presents a series of civil laws that became
known as the Mosaic legislation, and concludes with a
description of the building of the Tabernacle in the
wilderness.

Leviticus (Vayikra) contains the elaborate ritual and
ceremonies connected with the offering of sacrifices and
describes the functions of the Cohen and the Levite. It
also contains the dietary laws, laws pertaining to personal hygiene and public health, the laws of the Jubilee
Year (freedom of slaves), and a special chapter on ethical
conduct (Ch. 19).

Numbers (Bamidbor) deals with the period when the

Israelites in the wilderness were "numbered" and organized. It also contains the stories of the spies, of Korah's rebellion, of Balak and Balaam, of Moses' disobedience in smiting the rock, of the many wars which the Israelites fought during the forty years of their wandering.

Deuteronomy (D'vorim) repeats, to a large extent, the material of the previous four books. It also contains a number of additional laws, a series of moral teachings, and Moses' last message to his people.

2. NEVIIM (PROPHETS)

The second part of the Bible, composed of ten books, is divided into two parts:

A. *Neviim Rishonim* (Earlier Prophets), a collection of six historic books:

Joshua. This book gives the history of Joshua, the successor to Moses. It describes in detail the many wars which led to the conquest of Canaan, tells of the miracle at Gibeon, and concludes with the division of the land among the twelve tribes.

Judges. In this book is given the history of the unification of the tribes under leaders who were called "Judges." This early period in Jewish history, which lasted approximately three hundred years, may be divided into three periods, in each of which three judges were prominent. (1) Othniel, Ehud, Deborah; (2) Gideon, Abimelech, Jephtah; (3) Samson, Eli, Samuel.

Samuel I, gives the story of the birth, early training, and development of Samuel. Like Samson, Samuel was a Nazarite (dedicated to God), but unlike Samson, his strength was spiritual, not physical. In this book we are told how Samuel organized the "B'nai Ha-Neviim" (sons of the prophets), a prophetic guild of young enthusiasts. We are also told how the tribes of Israel asked for a king and how the kingdom was inaugurated under King Saul. Samuel I also tells of Saul's decline and David's rise in popular favor, of the friendship between David and Jonathan, of Saul's attempt to kill David, of the tragic death of Saul and Jonathan on Mt. Gilboa.

Samuel II. This book begins with David's lament for Jonathan and continues with a description of David's formation of a kingdom in southern Palestine (Hebron) and his later rule over a united kingdom. It then tells of David's achievements as a warrior, as a poet and musician, and as the builder of the city of Jerusalem. It also tells of Absalom's unsuccessful rebellion and the other events in the life of David.

Kings I. This book contains the history of King Solomon, of the expansion of his kingdom, of the building and dedication of the Temple at Jerusalem. It also gives the events which brought about the division of the kingdom after Solomon's death into Judah, under Rehoboam, and Israel, under Jeroboam. The worship of Baal which became popular in the days of Ahab and Jezebel, and the courage and heroism of Elijah, the champion of God's cause, are described. The book also gives us short biographies of the kings of Judah, Asa and Jehoshaphat, who, unlike the kings of Israel, were righteous and God-fearing rulers.

Kings II. In this book is the complete history of the kings of Israel and Judah, the activities of the prophetic guild (sons of the prophets), and the miracles of Elisha. It tells of Joash, the boy king, who repaired the Temple and encouraged worship therein; of Jeroboam, the second, the powerful king of Israel who conquered Assyria and annexed Damascus to his kingdom; of the wicked orgies in Damascus which caused Amos to attack the ruling classes and plead for justice to the oppressed; of the destruction of the kingdom of Israel by Assyria (722 B. C. E.). The book then tells of Hezekiah, the noble king of Judah, who heeded the counsel of the prophet Isaiah; of the wicked Menasseh who encouraged the worship of idols;

of King Josiah who found in the Temple a hidden manuscript of one of the books of the Torah (Deuteronomy)
and had it read before the people. It concludes with the
conquest of Judah by the Babylonians and the destruction of the Temple (586 B. C. E.).

    B. *Neviim Achronim* (Latter Prophets). Four books of
        sermons and messages by Israel's heroes of the
        spirit—the prophets:

Isaiah, the book that gives the biography and exhorta-
tions of Isaiah, the statesman prophet, the champion of
the common people, the friend, yet severe critic, of the
kings of Judah, especially of Hezekiah. Isaiah denounced
popular indulgence in ceremonies and minimized the
importance of sacrifices. The latter portion of the book
of Isaiah, beginning with chapter forty, is attributed to
"Deutero Isaiah," an anonymous prophet who lived in
Babylonia as an exile and predicted the coming of the
Messiah and the return of the Judeans to the Holy Land.

Jeremiah, the book which gives the messages and experiences of Jeremiah, the great patriot. The biblical "man
of sorrows," he predicted the fall of the kingdom of Judah and the destruction of Jerusalem, and lived to see
the fulfillment of his sad prophecies and the suffering
of his people (586 B. C. E.). His dirges and "Lamentations" express the agonies of a nation in ruins.

Ezekiel, the book about the prophet of the Babylonian
exile who assumed leadership over his people there. He
comforted those who, in moments of despair, "wept by
the rivers of Babylon" and refused "to sing the songs of
the Lord in a strange land" (Ps. 137). Ezekiel told his
brethren that even though they no longer lived in the
land of the Bible, it was their duty to abide by the laws
of the Bible, and he saw the establishment of the syna-

gogue (Greek for assembly place) in the Babylonian exile. His vision of the "dry bones" (Ch. 37) revived the spirits of a people who had lost all hope in the future. Ezekiel not only prophesied the rebuilding of the Temple at Jerusalem, but even designed plans for the new building.

Book of Twelve, the experiences and messages of twelve prophets included in one book. They are called the "Twelve Minor Prophets" not because they were of minor importance, but because the amount of their writings was small, ranging from one chapter (Obadiah) to fourteen chapters (Hosea and Zecheriah). Practically all of the twelve "minor" prophets were men of great vision and moral courage.

1. *Hosea,* a prophet in the kingdom of Israel, deplored the lack of loyalty of the bride (Israel) to her betrothed (God). The Haphtorah of Sabbath "Shuvah," beginning with the familiar words, "Return, O Israel, unto the Lord, thy God" (14:2), is Hosea's most famous appeal to the people of Israel for greater loyalty to the God of love and mercy. To Hosea "God is love."

2. *Joel,* of Judah, was a prophet of evil tidings who warned the people to be prepared for the coming of the "Day of the Lord." He also foresaw the coming of a plague of locusts. However, he assured the people that even in times of disaster "God is in the midst of Israel" (2:27).

3. *Amos,* the stern preacher of social justice, was a native of Judah who prophesied in Israel (Ab. 800 B. C. E.). Before Amos, professional soothsayers (sons of the prophets) gave prophetic messages to individuals, for a consideration, but Amos

inaugurated a new type of prophecy in which the people, and the nation, were targets of public attack. When told to go to Judah and there "eat bread" (make a living) through prophecy, Amos replied, "I am neither a prophet nor a son of a prophet. I am a farmer and a herdman, and God took me from the flock and said unto me, 'Go, prophesy to my people Israel'" (7:14). He assailed the vices of the rich and powerful, and championed the rights of the poor and the downtrodden. "God is justice!" was the message of Amos.

4. *Obadiah,* in a single chapter, rebuked the children of Esau (Edomites) for their cruelty to the children of Jacob. He foretold the doom of the Edomites and of the other nations attacking the people of Israel. Obadiah may be described as the voice of vengeance.

5. *Jonah,* a contemporary of Amos, lived in the northern kingdom (Israel). He was ordered by God to tell the people of Nineveh, a Gentile city, to repent of their evil ways lest they be utterly destroyed. Jonah, who disliked his mission, fled to the sea, was thrown off his boat, swallowed by a fish, and then thrown on a lonely beach. He finally went to Nineveh and proclaimed God's message. The people there heard his words, repented of their evil deeds, and were forgiven by God. The book of Jonah tells us that God is kind and forgiving toward all people, Jew and Gentile alike.

6. *Micah,* like Amos, was a peasant prophet and a social reformer who preached in the kingdom of Judah. He upbraided the priests and the leaders

of the people; he assailed the ritual of sacrifices; and he gave us the well-known formula for religious living, "He told thee, O man, what is good; and what does the Lord require of thee? Only to do justice, to love mercy, and to walk humbly with thy God" (6:8).

7. *Nahum* denounced the city of Nineveh, the capital of Assyria, because of its people's constant attacks on Judah. He foretold the fall and complete destruction of this "city of blood" and the vindication of the popular proverb that "he who takes to the sword shall perish by the sword."

8. *Habbakuk* was a philosopher prophet who asked, "Why do the righteous suffer and the wicked prosper?" when he saw the growing power of Babylonia and the decline of Judah. His third chapter is a beautiful hymn, extolling the glories of God. Habbakuk gave us, according to the Talmud, the shortest formula of religion—"The Righteous shall live by his Faith" (2:4).

9. *Zephaniah,* a prophet in Judah, lived in the period of King Josiah who, after finding the book of Deuteronomy, instituted many reforms in accordance with its commandments. Like Joel, Zephaniah spoke at length of the coming "Day of the Lord," or "Judgment Day." He predicted the doom and fall of Jerusalem, but placed his hopes in the "remnant of Israel."

10. *Haggai*—the first prophet of the "Return." When Judeans returned to Jerusalem from the Babylonian exile (536 B. C. E.), their first ambition was to rebuild the Temple in accordance with the plans drawn up by Ezekiel. The building of the Temple was begun, but was frequently interrupted be-

cause the people were more interested in building homes for themselves than in building a House for God. Then Haggai appeared on the scene and asked, "Is it a time for you to dwell in your ceiled houses, while this house lieth waste?" (1:4). Inspired by Haggai's message, the people again took up the building of the Temple.

11. *Zechariah*—the second prophet of the "Return." Like Haggai, Zechariah urged the people to proceed with the work of rebuilding the Temple. He also restored the people's confidence in the future of the nation and in the establishment of God's kingdom. Zechariah visualized the day when the tribal God of Israel would be the universal God. "And the Lord shall be King over all the earth; in that day shall the Lord be One, and His name One" (14:9). Zechariah summarized his formula of religion in the words, "Truth, justice, and peace practice in your gates" (8:16).

12. *Malachi*—the third prophet of the "Return," prophesied in the days of Ezra, about 450 B. C. E. With him prophecy deteriorated and came to an end. Unlike the other prophets, he stressed the importance of sacrifices and rebuked the priests who offered animals of inferior quality as sacrifices. Unlike the other prophets, too, he asked the people to contribute to the Temple treasury and promised them divine blessings in return. Malachi predicted that the prophet Elijah would come to Israel prior to the coming of the "Great Day of the Lord." He also pleaded for universal brotherhood with the words, "Have we not all one father? Hath not one God created us?" (2:10).

3. CHESSUVIM

Chessuvim, or Kethubim, known as "Writings" or "Hagiagrapha," is a collection of thirteen different books, all of them considered worthy of inclusion into the Holy Writ. They may be divided into the following three groups:

1. MEDITATION AND PHILOSOPHY

Psalms. The book of Psalms contains one hundred and fifty hymns of praise and meditation, expressing the glories of God and man's implicit faith in His justice and mercy.

David, the "sweet singer of Israel," was the first to write these inspiring poems and put them to music. He popularized them and made them the basis of public worship. In the days of Solomon, additional psalms were written and music for them was composed by the directors of music in the Temple. In the period of the first Temple, in the days of the Babylonian exile, and in the early days of the second Temple other psalms were written and made a part of Jewish liturgy. Today, the psalms not only form the greater part of Jewish prayers, but are sung and recited in the houses of worship of many religions in all parts of the world.

Proverbs is a collection of maxims, epigrams, and words of wisdom, the authorship of which is contributed to King Solomon. The Proverbs contain advice for man's guidance; they emphasize the importance of young people's avoiding temptation and heeding the admonitions of parents and teachers. The last chapter of the book describes the excellent qualities of the "Eshes Chayil" —the valiant woman.

Job is a book of religious philosophy which reads like a drama. Its introductory story is told in a prologue; the major part of the book contains a series of debates and discussions on all phases of religious belief and interpretation; the concluding events are given in an epilogue.

In the prologue we are told that in a mythical place called Uz there lived a man by the name of Job who was a God-fearing, prosperous man and the patriarch of a large household. He was tested by God, at the instigation of Satan. One misfortune after another befell him as his children were killed, his possessions lost, and his body afflicted with physical suffering. He accepted these acts of God with pious resignation. "God hath given, God hath taken, blessed be the name of God."

Four of his friends came to console him in his misery, and a debate followed, with each of the friends accusing Job of heresy, giving different reasons. When Job broke down under the strain and rebelled against God's injustice to him and to other people suffering without cause, he was mercilessly rebuked by his friends. They insisted that he was being punished because he was a sinner, even though Job enumerated his ethical deeds and his acts of piety and kindness. The debate then became vehement on the subjects of what is wisdom and what is folly, what is virtue and what is sin.

The epilogue tells us that the voice of God, coming from a whirlwind, refuted Job's accusers and proclaimed his innocence. Job lived to see his house restored to its former glory. He once more became the father of a large family and the possessor of great wealth.

2. SACRED SCROLLS

The Song of Songs contains a series of dialogues between a youthful lover, presumably King Solomon, and a coy shepherdess, named Shulamith. According to the sages of the Talmud these dialogues are mystical and allegorical conversations between God (the groom) and Israel (the bride), intended to remind the Jewish people of the days of Sinai when God and Israel declared their love for each other and were subsequently wedded. The book is read in the synagogue during the week of Passover, the festive period of spring and joy. Many devout Jews chant the Song of Songs every Friday.

Ruth. This book tells the story of Ruth, a Moabitish woman, who left her people and her religion to become a convert to Judaism. Her loyalty and devotion to Naomi, her mother-in-law, are beautifully expressed in the words, "Entreat me not to leave thee . . ." (1:16). In the harvest season Ruth joined the poor of the town and picked up "gleanings," ears of corn accidentally dropped by the reapers. Boaz, a wealthy man and a near relative of Naomi, married Ruth, and she became the ancestress of the house of David. The Book of Ruth, featuring a harvest season and Ruth's acceptance of Judaism, is read on Shavuos, the festival of the first ripe fruits (Bikkurim) and the anniversary of Israel's acceptance of the Ten Commandments.

Lamentations are, as the name implies, a collection of wailings and laments. They were written by Jeremiah, the "prophet of sorrow," who predicted, and later witnessed, the fall of Jerusalem and the destruction of the Temple (586 B. C. E.). The Book of Lamentations is read on Tisha B'Ab (9th of Ab), the anniversary of the destruction of both the first and second Temples.

Ecclesiastes, also known by its Hebrew name of "Koheleth," contains a series of philosophic reflections on the vanity of life and the futility of man's ambitions. "Vanity of vanities, saith Koheleth; vanity of vanities, all is vanity" (1:2). It is a collection of sad truths, of words of wisdom permeated by pessimism; its authorship is attributed to Solomon. One of the sages of the Talmud ventures the opinion that King Solomon, in his early youth, wrote the "Song of Songs"; in his prime of life, he wrote the book of "Proverbs"; in his declining days, he wrote "Koheleth." Ecclesiastes contains many quotations contrary to the accepted beliefs of Judaism, but it redeems itself in its last words, "The end of the matter, all having been heard: fear God, and keep His commandments; for this is the whole man" (12:13). The Book of Ecclesiastes is read during the week of Succos, when falling leaves announce the approaching death of field and forest.

Esther is the book which gives in detail the dramatic story of the plottings of Haman and of Israel's deliverance through the intervention of Mordecai and Esther. The Book of Esther is read on Purim. Although every one of the sacred scrolls is called in Hebrew a Megillah, the Book of Esther is popularly known as *the* Megillah.

3. Biography and History

Daniel presents the biography of a wise and God-fearing Jew who was adviser to the kings of Babylon during the period of the Babylonian exile (586–536 B. C. E.). Although the Book of Daniel, written partly in Hebrew and partly in Aramaic, is replete with religious fervor,

miracles, and prophecies, it is not given a place among
the books of the prophets. In the Christian arrangement
of the Old Testament, Daniel is listed as one of the major
prophets—Isaiah, Jeremiah, Ezekiel, Daniel—, but the
Jewish Bible places the Book of Daniel in a position of
minor importance among the "Writings." Daniel's miraculous escape from the lions' den, his explanation of
the king's dream, his interpretation of the mysterious
handwriting on the wall, and his prediction of the conquest of Babylonia by the Persians are important features of the book. However, the sages of the Talmud
recommend that the Book of Daniel be considered as
history or biography and not as prophecy, because of the
doubtful truth of its contents and the anonymity of its
author.

Ezra contains the biography of one of the great men in
Jewish history. Ezra, the "Scribe," was a scholar, a fiery
orator, and a man of vision; he is frequently called the
second Moses, for "Moses gave the laws, Ezra enforced
them." A native of Babylonia, his interests were nevertheless in Palestine where the struggling pioneers were
rebuilding the national Jewish homeland. He inspired
the Jews of Babylonia, who had grown prosperous in
exile, to give money and encouragement to the "builders
of Zion," and finally gathered together a large sum of
money and a great number of people (some five thousand souls) for an expedition to Jerusalem (about 450
B. C. E.). Arriving there, he assembled the people in the
Temple area and ordered them to study the Torah, to
obey the laws of Moses, and to send away their heathen
wives. The people promised under oath to do his bidding, and they did. To carry out his reforms, Ezra organized an assembly of elders, arranged to have passages of

the Torah read at public worship, and began a collection
of all available manuscripts of sacred contents, the beginning of the compilation of the Bible. Ezra saved the
Torah, preserved the sanctity of the Jewish home, and
snatched from oblivion the spiritual heritage of the Jewish people.

Nehemiah gives the autobiography of a great leader. It
was either during the declining days of Ezra, or soon
after Ezra's death, that reports of the sad plight of the
Jews of Jerusalem reached Nehemiah, a man of wisdom
and power, who occupied a position of trust in the court
of the Persian king. Having secured the authority to act
as representative of the king of Persia, Nehemiah came to
Jerusalem (about 380 B. C. E.) and instituted there a
practical program of reconstruction. He subdued the
Samaritans, the enemies from within, and rebuilt the
walls and outer defenses of the city against attacks from
without. He regulated commerce, established industries,
and organized a small army. A deeply religious man,
Nehemiah enforced the spiritual reforms introduced by
Ezra. The Talmud criticizes Nehemiah because he asks
that God reward him for what he has done—"Remember unto me, O my God, for good, all that I have done
for this people" (5:19). Nevertheless, the piety and sin-
cerity of Nehemiah have been recognized, and one of
his prayers (9:6) is recited daily by the observant Jew.

Chronicles I is a book of history summarizing the events
of the Bible from Adam to Solomon. The first ten chapters of the book give names and places, but no cohesive
stories. From the eleventh chapter to the end (twenty-
nine chapters) is given a complete history of the life of
King David.

Chronicles II gives a detailed description of the life and

accomplishments of King Solomon and then presents
biographies of the rulers of the divided kingdom. It gives
scanty attention to the kings of Israel, mentioning only
Jeroboam and Ahab, but tells at length about the kings
of Judah. The book concludes with the text of the decla-
ration issued by Cyrus (536 B. C. E.), allowing the Jews
in the Babylonian exile to return to Jerusalem, if they
so desired.

The compilation of the books of the Bible was begun
by Ezra (about 450 B. C. E.) and continued by the Men
of the Great Assembly, or The Great Synagogue. The
sages of the Mishnah (Tanaim) had many debates on the
question as to which of the available manuscripts should
be included in the sacred collection, and finally the
Bible Canon, or "Holy Writ," was closed at about the
time of the destruction of the second Temple (70 C. E.).
The process of editing the Bible and of correcting text-
ual errors became known as "Massorah," the Hebrew
word for "tradition."

The Bible, the primary source of Judaism, is the book
which created and preserved the Jewish people. In it are
all the elements which contributed to the development
of civilization—history, religion, poetry, wisdom, laws.
It is the basic foundation of the monotheistic religions
of the world. It is Israel's eternal contribution to humanity.

"Apocrypha" (Greek for "hidden") is the name given to
a collection of books not included in the Holy Scriptures.
The reason for the exclusion of those books is not

known. The Talmud speaks of them as "S'forim G'nu-zim" (books to be hidden). The Apocrypha contains, among others, Maccabees I and Maccabees II, which give the history and background of the events which led to the Maccabean victory over the Syrian Hellenists and to the rededication (Chanukah) of the second Temple in the year 165 B. C. E. In some Christian Bibles the Apocrypha is inserted between the Old Testament and the New Testament.

II. THE TALMUD

The second source of Judaism is that famous collection of books known as the Talmud, its name meaning learning, or study. Commentaries upon the Torah have occupied the minds of our rabbis for many generations, and the Talmud is the greatest and most voluminous work which explains "Holy Writ." "Talmud" is the composite name of two great works: (1) Mishnah, (2) Gemarah.

1. *The Mishnah.* The Mishnah is called "Oral Law" to distinguish it from the "Written Law" of the Torah. At about 150 B. C. E., soon after the rededication of the Temple by the Maccabees, the Jews of Palestine and of Babylonia threw themselves zealously into the study of the Torah. Ezra and the Men of the Great Assembly had edited the Torah and put it to script, but the comments on it were not put in writing, lest they be considered as holy as the Torah itself. These comments became known as the "Oral Law," they were committed to memory and handed down from generation to generation. The word "Mishnah" means diligent study and repetition. Some of the laws of the Mishnah were based directly on the commands of the Torah; others were adopted because they had been actually in force for a long time. The "Tanaim," authors of the Mishnah, maintained large schools and presided over legislative assemblies; they became famous for their erudition and for their discipline. Those great scholars and patriots saved Judaism in a critical period of its history.

In the year 200 C. E., after three hundred and fifty years of studying "by heart," Rabbi Judah, the Prince, was bold enough to disregard tradition and put the commentaries and decisions of the Mishnah into writing. By compiling and editing the Mishnah, Rabbi Judah actually created the first code of laws of Judaism. The Mishnah is divided into six parts:

1. *Z'raim* (seeds). This section contains laws pertaining to agriculture, to planting and harvesting, to land purchases, and to the rights of the poor. It also gives different prayers for the enjoyment of food.

2. *Mo'ed* (festivals). This tractate of the Mishnah deals with the observance of the Sabbath, the holy days, the customs prevalent in the land at the time of the second Temple. It also states the duties of pilgrims in the observance of the festivals.

3. *Nashim* (women). This section gives a series of laws pertaining to marriage and divorce; it also gives instructions about the Levirate marriage (marrying a childless widow of a brother), the Chalitza (see "Customs"), and about domestic relations.

4. *N'zikin* (damages). This order of the Mishnah is a complete code of civil and criminal laws, covering all matters of property rights.

5. *Kodshim* (sacred things). A complete description of the sacrifices in the second Temple and of the many rituals observed on various occasions.

6. *Taharos* (purifications). This order describes all types of hygienic laws, religious ablutions, and the laws of the Mikvah, or ritual bath.

The laws of the Torah are scattered and disorganized.

Their first systematic arrangement appeared when the Mishnah was compiled and written.

2. *The Gemarah.* As soon as the Mishnah made its appearance, comments upon it began to pour in from all parts of the Jewish world. With a written manuscript before them, the sages of Palestine and Babylonia began to dissect it and to discuss every word of it, producing a tremendous amount of supplementary material. This material was compiled under the name of Gemarah, which means "completion." The scholars who created the Gemarah are known as "Amoraim."

The Gemarah was compiled at about 500 C. E., three hundred years after the completion of the Mishnah. Though a commentary on the Mishnah, it differs greatly from the work upon which it comments. The Mishnah is written in pure Hebrew, while the Gemarah is a mixture of Hebrew and Aramaic. The Mishnah is almost entirely a code of laws, but the Gemarah is divided between Halacha (laws) and Agadda (adages, fables, and homiletics). The Mishnah is small in form and limited in scope, while the Gemarah is a vast treasure house of legal sagacity, of literature, of folklore, and of religious research.

The Talmud—Mishnah and Gemarah combined—is an important source of Judaism because it is a collection of Jewish laws and of rabbinical interpretations based on the Torah. Many of the laws of Judaism were directly ordered in the Torah (Mid'oraisso), while others were established by the rabbis of the Talmud (Mid'-rabonon). That the laws of the Talmud are important is evident from the fact that the Karaites of the eighth and ninth centuries were excommunicated from the

House of Israel because they clung literally to the laws of the Torah and rejected the decisions of the rabbis of the Talmud. Since the days of the Karaites, the people of Israel have accepted the Talmud as an authoritative source of Judaism. There is a Jerusalem edition of the Talmud and a Babylonian edition, but the latter is by far the more important work. Whenever the word "Talmud" is mentioned, it usually refers to the Babylonian edition.

III. THE CODES OF JEWISH LAWS

The Torah contains many laws—religious, civil, criminal, ceremonial, ethical. There were times in Jewish history when these laws were rigidly adhered to, but there were also times when "every man did what seemed right in his own eyes." In some periods the "Laws of Moses" were considered fixed and unchangeable, while in others the "Written Law" was modified and even changed by the "Oral Law" of the Talmud. It became evident some hundreds of years ago that the laws of the Torah, interpreted in various ways by the rabbis of the Talmud, lacked finality and should be codified, by leading rabbis, for the guidance of the Jewish people. The following are the codes of laws that may be considered the authoritative sources of Judaism.

1. *Shaalos U'tshuvos,* usually translated as "Responsa." From the sixth century through the twelfth, there were many rabbinical authorities who wrote down all the difficult problems brought to their attention and also stated the answers (Responsa) they gave to these questions. These opinions of rabbinical dignitaries on actual cases were soon recognized as precedents and were followed by other authorities and by the Jewish people at large. Many books on "Responsa" interpreted various phases of Jewish legalism and became the codes of Judaism during that period.

2. *Mishneh Torah* (Second Law) by Maimonides. This code of laws, also known as "Yad Hachazakah" (strong

hand), was compiled by Maimonides in the twelfth century. The Hebrew name of Maimonides was Rabbi Moses ben Maimon, and he is known in Jewish literature as RaMBaM, a composite word derived from the first initials of his name. Maimonides, whose name has been frequently mentioned in this book, was not only the outstanding Jewish physician of the Middle Ages, but also the first codifier of Jewish law as well as the first man to write an exhaustive book on Jewish philosophy. Maimonides was familiar with Greek culture, with Roman law, and with every form of Jewish legalism contained in the Talmud and in the "Responsa." His "Mishneh Torah" which codified every aspect of Jewish life—theology, ethics, ritual, and jurisprudence—was a perfect code of Jewish laws, properly arranged and systematized. It was soon recognized as the most authoritative work on Judaism, and its decisions are still recognized, though to a limited degree, in our days.

3. *Shulchan Aruch* (Prepared Table), a code of Jewish laws largely modeled after that of Maimonides. Its author, Rabbi Joseph Caro, lived in Safed, Palestine, where he completed the "Shulchan Aruch" in the year 1570.

The "Shulchan Aruch" is based primarily on the laws of the Talmud, but it takes many liberties in reversing the interpretations there and also differs, in many instances, from the opinions of Maimonides. It makes use of all the decisions rendered in the "Responsa" which appeared between the twelfth and the sixteenth centuries. It not only codifies the laws of the Torah and of the Talmud, but also gives decisions on the religious importance of all the observances and institutions that developed in Israel during the post-Talmudic period.

The "Shulchan Aruch" is now recognized throughout the Jewish world as the standard code of Jewish laws.

―――――――――――

"And now, O Israel, what doth the Lord thy God require of thee, but to fear the Lord thy God, to walk in all His ways, and to love Him, and to serve the Lord thy God with all thy heart and with all thy soul" (Deut. 10:12).

BIBLIOGRAPHY

THE BIBLE.

THE TALMUD, Babylonian edition.

MISHNEH TORAH, Moses Maimonides.

SHULCHAN ARUCH, Joseph Caro.

JEWISH ENCYCLOPEDIA, Funk and Wagnalls, New York.

THE UNIVERSAL JEWISH ENCYCLOPEDIA, University Press, New York.

ENCYCLOPEDIA OF JEWISH KNOWLEDGE, ed. J. DeHaas.

OZAR DINIM UMINHOGIM, ed. J. D. Eisenstein.

GUIDE TO THE PERPLEXED, Moses Maimonides.

IKKARIM, Joseph Albo.

THE PROPHETS AND THEIR TIMES, J. Powis Smith.

THE PROPHETS, Edward C. Baldwin.

WHAT WE JEWS BELIEVE, Samuel S. Cohon.

JEWISH THEOLOGY, Kaufmann Kohler.

THE ETHICS OF JUDAISM, Moritz Lazarus.

ETHICS OF THE FATHERS, J. Gorfinkle.

THE MESSIAH IDEA IN JEWISH HISTORY, Julius H. Greenstone.

THE JEWISH RELIGION, Michael Friedlander.

OUTLINES OF LIBERAL JUDAISM, Claude G. Montefiore.

THE RELIGION OF ISRAEL, Julius H. Greenstone.

JUDAISM AS A CIVILIZATION, Mordecai M. Kaplan.

JUDAISM AS CREED AND LIFE, Morris Joseph.

JEWISH CEREMONIES AND CUSTOMS, William Rosenau.

RELIGIONS OF DEMOCRACY (Judaism), Louis Finkelstein.

SOME ASPECTS OF RABBINIC THEOLOGY, Solomon Schechter.

GLOSSARY

This glossary is *not* a collection of biographies of Jewish leaders, past or present. It is merely a set of sketchy biographies of those personalities whose names appear in this volume.

Aaron, high priest, brother of Moses; presiding dignitary at the sacrifices in the Tabernacle; the first "Cohen," founder of the family of priests, or "Cohanim."

Abraham, the first of the three patriarchs, the father of the Hebrew race; faithful servant of God and lover of man. The law of circumcision, or "Bris," dates back to Abraham, and the ceremony is known as the Abrahamic Covenant.

Ahab, one of the kings of Israel. He introduced Baal worship at the instigation of his wicked wife, Jezebel; he persecuted the prophet Elijah.

Ahashverosh, the weak, vacillating king in the Book of Esther. History identifies him with Artaxerxes. In modern literature the name Ahashverosh has been given to Eugene Sue's mystical, but historically incorrect, "wandering Jew."

Akiba ben Joseph, known as Rabbi Akiba, born 50 C. E., martyred in 133. A leading "Tana" of the Mishnah, an authority on Jewish law, head of a large Talmud academy. He proclaimed Bar Kochba as the Messiah and supported the revolution which Bar Kochba led against the Romans and their emperor Hadrian. As spiritual head of the Jews of Palestine, he ordered his people to join the army of rebellion; he was seized by the Romans and tortured to death.

Albo, Joseph, Spanish rabbi and theologian, 1380 to 1444. Albo was a famous preacher and debater on religious subjects; he is chiefly known as the author of the book on Jewish fundamentals (Ikkarim).

Alexander, the Great, annexed Palestine to his vast kingdom. He entered Jerusalem in 332 B. C. E., not as a conqueror but as a friend of the Jewish people. He was received with great acclaim and his Greek ideology (Hellenism) became popular in Palestine.

Amos, a fearless and courageous prophet, champion of justice and defender of human rights; he preached in Damascus and in Samaria, about 800 B. C. E.

Antiochus, king of Syria, died 164 B. C. E.; the wicked tyrant who sought to destroy Judaism and to exterminate the Jewish people; his plans were frustrated by Judah Maccabee and his faithful followers.

Aristotle, a Greek philosopher of the fourth century B. C. E., influenced the Jewish mind more than any other Gentile thinker. According to Maimonides, the theories of Aristotle and those of Judaism coincide in many respects.

Bachya Ibn Pekuda. Jewish mystic and scholar who lived in Saragossa, Spain, in the eleventh century. He was the author of "Chovos Halevovos" (Duties of the Heart), the first book to give a complete and systematic presentation of Jewish ethics; his book is much quoted in the religious and homiletic literature of Judaism.

Bar Kochba, Simon, born in 90 C. E. In the year 132 he proclaimed himself the Messiah and started a holy war to free the Jews of Palestine from Roman domination. His claim to the Messiahship was substantiated by Rabbi Akiba and by most of the scholars of that age. His rebellion assumed large proportions and his army mounted to three hundred thousand men; after three years of severe fighting, Bar Kochba took refuge in the stronghold of Bethar where his army was defeated and he was killed, in 135 c. e.

Bezalel, the famous designer and builder of the Tabernacle in the desert. The Bible tells us that Bezallel was not only a resourceful architect, but also a skillful worker with all types of cloth and metal. His construction of the collapsible Tabernacle was, in his days, an outstanding feat of craftsmanship. His memory was recently honored when a Jewish art school, bearing the name of Bezallel, was established in Jerusalem.

Boaz, a wealthy farmer in Bethlehem, kinsman of Naomi; he married Ruth and became the progenitor of the House of David.

Caro (or Karo), Joseph, codifier of rabbinical Judaism, was born in Spain, 1488; died in Safed, Palestine, in 1575. After the expulsion of the Jews from Spain, in 1492, Caro went with his parents to Turkey. In 1535 he came to Safed where he joined a group of scholars and mystics. His fame spread rapidly and he was soon recognized as the outstanding authority on Jewish law. He codified all types of Jewish laws—civil, religious, and domestic; he arranged his codes in four volumes under the title "Shulchan Aruch" (Prepared Table). He based his decisions on all the rabbinical interpretations that were recorded since the days of the Mishnah; he also followed, to a large extent, the decisions made by Maimonides. Caro's "Shulchan Aruch" is now the universally recognized code of Jewish law.

Daniel, a post-biblical personality whose biography is recorded in the Book of Daniel, in the "Writings" division of the Bible. He presumably lived in the Babylonian exile (586–536 b. c. e.). It was long after his death that the history of his life was written by an anonymous author.

David, king of Judah (in Hebron), for seven years; king of the United Kingdom (in Jerusalem), for thirty-three years. He was a political leader and skilled warrior, also a musician and a poet. His history is recorded in Samuel I and Samuel II; also in Chronicles I.

Elijah, the mysterious figure who suddenly appeared on the scene and championed the cause of God against the worship of Baal. Elijah's courage in denouncing wickedness, his firm stand against an overwhelming majority, and his flight heavenward in a fiery chariot made him a mysterious figure in Jewish life. He is expected to come again, as the forerunner of the Messiah.

Elisha, the miracle man in the early days of prophecy. He was the favorite disciple and successor of Elijah. Elisha was the supporter and protector of the young enthusiasts who were organized into a prophetic guild (sons of the prophets).

Esther, also known by the Hebrew name "Hadassah." She rose to fame as the winner in a beauty contest, but proved to be a serious minded and deeply religious woman. Her intervention in behalf of the Jewish people at the peril of her life marks an interesting chapter in the history of the Jewish people, as recorded in the Book of Esther.

Eve, the first woman in the world, the "mother of all living." According to the biblical version, she enticed man to sin and was the indirect cause of the curse which brought death to mankind. That act of Eve may be the reason why women were placed in an inferior position in early Jewish (and Christian) history.

Ezekiel, the outstanding prophet in the period of the Babylonian exile (586–536 B. C. E.). He disapproved of many ceremonies in Jewish life, minimized the importance of the sacrifices, and championed the cause of ethical Judaism. He also advocated the theory of personal responsibility in religion. He gave hope and courage to the people in exile, assured them of the coming of the

Messiah, and laid plans for the rebuilding of the Temple.

Ezra, the "Scribe," was born in Babylonia where he acquired scholarship and wealth. He came to Jerusalem, about 450 B. C. E., and instituted a number of reforms which were desperately needed at that time. He actually saved the program of the "Return" and preserved Judaism, and the Jewish people, for the generations to come.

Gedaliah, the man who was appointed by the king of Babylon to act as governor of Jerusalem after the city had been ransacked and destroyed by the Babylonians. The people of Jerusalem, defeated after three years of resistance, were bitter and rebellious. They assassinated Gedaliah and brought upon themselves the wrath of Babylonia. The massacre of the Jews which followed was so bloody that the people of Jerusalem remembered the day of Gedaliah's assassination and proclaimed it a day of prayer and fasting. The "Fast of Gedaliah," occurring on the day after Rosh Hashanah, is still observed to this day.

Habakkuk, one of the minor prophets whose messages are recorded, in three chapters, and incorporated in the Book of Twelve.

Hadassah (See "Esther").

Hadrian, Roman emperor (117–138) who oppressed the Jews of Palestine. He suppressed the Bar Kochba rebellion and laid waste the city of Jerusalem.

Haggai, first prophet of the "Return"; he urged the people to rebuild the Temple. His prophecies, consisting of two chapters, are recorded in the Book of Twelve.

Hannah, the mother of Samuel, author of a beautiful poem which is read as the Haphtorah of the first day of Rosh Hashanah (Samuel I, Chapter 2).

Hannah, the mother of seven sons and one of the heroines of the Chanukah story. According to the Talmud, Hannah encouraged each of her seven sons to reject the offer of King Antiochus and to accept the fate of martyrdom for the glory of the God of Israel.

Hillel. Famous scholar and educator, founder of the school called after him. He lived in Jerusalem in the days of King Herod (about 40–10 B. C. E.), and was the Nassi (prince) of the Jewish community of Palestine. He was an authority on Jewish law, a man of kindness and patience, and the author of many sayings and epigrams.

Hosea, one of the minor prophets whose experiences and messages are recorded, in fourteen chapters, and given the first place in the Book of Twelve.

Ibn Gabirol, Solomon, poet and philosopher; born in Malaga, Spain, in 1020, died in Valencia, 1060. He was one of the great intellectuals of the Jewish "Golden Era" in Spain. Author of "Mekor Chayim" (Fountain of Life) and of a number of poems that are now included in the Jewish liturgy.

Isaac, the son of Abraham, second of the three patriarchs. His wife was Rebecca, the kind maiden of the Bible. Isaac had two sons, Jacob and Esau.

Isaiah, the outstanding prophet in the Kingdom of Judah. The period of his prophecy covers a period of about fifty years (750–700 B. C. E.). Though an aristocrat and a royal adviser, he was the champion of the common people. His ideal of religion was to have man abandon the "wickedness" within him and to emphasize the "holiness" within him; he urged his people to imitate God who is the "source of holiness"; he constantly spoke of God as the "Holy One of Israel." The book bearing Isaiah's name is listed among the major prophets.

Isaiah (Deutero), the second, or latter, Isaiah whose identity remains unknown, lived in the Babylonian exile and predicted the coming of the Messiah. His beautiful and inspiring messages are recorded in the Book of Isaiah, beginning with chapter forty.

Jacob, the son of Isaac, third of the three patriarchs. By purchasing the "Birthright" from his brother Esau, Jacob became the successor to his father's household and title. He was also given the name of Israel, "champion of God." He was the father of twelve sons who later became known as the twelve tribes. He also adopted the two sons of Joseph, Menasseh and Ephraim. He died in Egypt, but was buried in the Cave of Machpelah, in Hebron.

Jeremiah, a prophet in the Kingdom of Judah. He predicted the fall of the kingdom and warned the people of the approaching doom. He was a great patriot, constantly seeking the welfare of his people. Like Isaiah, he denounced the ritual of the sacrifices and sought to improve the ethical standards of his people. When Jerusalem was captured by the Babylonians and the Temple lay in ruins, Jeremiah wrote the "Lamentations." His experiences and prophecies are recorded in the book bearing his name.

Jeroboam, a descendant of the tribe of Ephraim, raised a rebellion after the death of King Solomon, divided the kingdom, and became king of the northern Kingdom of Israel. He introduced the revolutionary slogan, "To thy tents, O Israel!" He was a wicked man who led his people to the worship of idolatry.

Jezebel, the wicked wife of King Ahab. She urged the people of Israel to worship Baal, supported a large number of men who called themselves prophets of Baal, and summoned these men to meet Elijah on Mt. Carmel. She met with a tragic end, as predicted by Elijah.

Job, the tragic figure of the Bible who suffered physical and mental agonies because of the intrigues of Satan. The Book of Job is a classic in the field of religious philosophy.

Jochanan ben Zakai. Palestinian "Tana," founder of the famous academy at Jabneh, or Jamnia, died about 80 C. E. When Jerusalem was about to fall, the Roman emperor Vespasian made a statement that he would grant any request that Jochanan would make. The modest request of Jochanan was, "Give me Jabneh and her scholars." The petition was granted; Jochanan saved his academy of learning and thus laid the foundation for the rebuilding of Jewish life through the study of the Torah.

Joel, one of the minor prophets, lived in Judah, but the exact time of his prophecy is undetermined; his words are recorded, in four chapters, in the Book of Twelve.

Jonah, a prophet in the Kingdom of Israel. His strange experiences and his messages are recorded, in four chapters, in the Book of Twelve.

Joseph, Morris, Rabbi and author, born in London, 1848, died in London, 1930; minister of West London Synagogue. Joseph is best known as the author of "Judaism as Creed and Life," a book that is quite popular in England.

Joshua, the successor of Moses, was a descendant of Ephraim. As one of the twelve spies, he joined Caleb in bringing in a favorable report about the Promised Land; he led the Israelites in their battles against their enemies during the period of the wilderness. At the death of Moses, Joshua took over the leadership; he conquered the nations of Palestine and divided the land among the twelve tribes.

Judah, the fourth son of Jacob, the leader among his brothers. The tribe of Judah later became the Kingdom of Judah, surviving the fall of the Kingdom of Israel and the disintegration of the "lost" ten tribes. Now, practically all the Jews of the world are descendants of Judah. As Judah was compared to a lion by his father, the Lion of Judah has become one of the symbols of the Jewish people.

Judah, rabbi and "Nassi" (prince) was born about 135 c. e., died about 220. The title "Nassi" (prince) was given to him as the head of the Jewish community in Palestine, a title which was previously held by Hillel. Rabbi Judah compiled and edited the "Mishnah," a collection of Jewish laws based on the Torah; he put to script the rabbinical interpretations which constituted the "Oral Law." The Mishnah forms the first part of the Talmud.

Judah Halevy, philosopher and foremost Hebrew poet since the Bible. Born in Toledo, Spain, about 1080, died either in Egypt or in Palestine, about 1143. Scholar, mystic, and lover of Zion. He expressed in beautiful poetry the yearnings of the Jewish soul; his "Odes to Zion" are outstanding pieces of Hebrew literature. Halevy's "Kuzari" gives a series of religious beliefs as presented before the king of the "Khazars," by leaders of the Christian, Mohammedan, and Jewish faiths. The book concludes that the Jewish presentation was given preference.

Kaplan, Mordecai M., rabbi, philosopher, educator; born in 1861, now living in New York. Professor of homiletics at the Jewish Theological Seminary and dean of its Teachers' Institute. He is the founder and leader of the Reconstructionist movement in Judaism. Author of many books; his "Judaism as a Civilization" contains a complete presentation of his philosophy of Judaism.

Kohler, Kaufmann, rabbi and theologian; born in Germany, 1843, died in New York, 1926. An extraordinary scholar, a prolific writer; the leader of Reform Judaism in America for over half a century. He was rabbi in Detroit, in Chicago, and in New York; in 1903 he became president of the Union Hebrew College in Cincinnati. Of his many books, "Jewish Theology" occupies the most important place.

Lazarus, Emma, American Jewish poetess, born in New York, 1849, died 1887. Her best known poem, "The

New Colossus," is placed on the base of the Statue of Liberty. Her most popular Jewish poem is "The Banner of the Jew."

Maccabeus, Judah, leader of the successful rebellion against the Syrians and against Hellenism. He defeated the enemy and rededicated the Temple to the service of God in 165 B. C. E.; he is the hero of the Chanukah story.

Maimonides, Moses, also known by the Hebrew name of RaMBaM, the initial letters of Rabbi Moses Ben Maimon. Born in Cordova, Spain, 1135; died in Cairo, Egypt, 1204. Physician, philosopher, and greatest Talmudist of the Middle Ages. Author of the thirteen principles of faith, or creeds, of Judaism (Anni Maamin); author of the "Moreh Nevuchim" (Guide to the Perplexed), a book on Jewish philosophy; also author of "Mishneh Torah," or "Yad Hachazakah," a complete code of Jewish laws based on Torah and Talmud. Maimonides has frequently been called the "third Moses" (Moses, Ezra, Maimonides).

Malachi, the last of the prophets, lived in Jerusalem in the days of Ezra (about 450 B. C. E.). His messages, in three chapters, are contained in the last book of the Book of Twelve.

Mattathias, a priest of the Hasmonean family, lived in the town of Modin where he started the Maccabean rebellion against Syria.

Menasseh, king of Judah, was the wicked son of a noble father. His father, King Hezekiah, was so religious and noble a man that the Talmud speaks of him as the "Messiah"; Menasseh, on the other hand, was an idol worshiper, a godless and cruel man. His life's history is related in Kings II, Chapter 21.

Menasseh ben Israel. Dutch rabbi, born in 1604, became rabbi of Amsterdam in 1627. Scholar, linguist, orator, diplomat. In 1655 he went to London, had several conferences with Oliver Cromwell, and succeeded in obtaining permission for the re-admission of Jews into England, the country from which they had been expelled in 1290.

Micah, a peasant prophet who prophesied in Judah. He was a disciple and great admirer of Isaiah. His experiences and messages are recorded, in seven chapters, in the collection of the Book of Twelve.

Miriam, a prophetess, sister of Moses and Aaron. She led the women of Israel in singing and dancing after the crossing of the Red Sea. She was the leader of the women of Israel in the early period of the wilderness.

Mohammed (570–632), founder of the religion known as Mohammedanism or Islam.

Mordecai, a descendant of Judah and an exile from Palestine, lived in Persia and was the foster father of Esther. He refused to bow to Haman, for which he and his people were condemned to die; he maintained contact with Esther and urged her to plead for her people. He finally attained honor and distinction in the Persian court.

Moses, prophet, law-giver, author; liberator of the children of Israel from Egyptian bondage. From the Jewish standpoint Moses was the outstanding personality of the Bible; he was the founder of Judaism and creator of the Jewish nation.

Nahum, a prophet in Judah, lived in the reign of Josiah. His book of three chapters, found in the Book of Twelve, is often called the "Oracle against Nineveh."

Nehemiah, patriot and leader. He came to the rescue of the struggling Judeans who were rebuilding the nation after the Babylonian exile. He rebuilt the walls and outer defenses of Jerusalem and organized a program of economic stabilization; a book bearing his name is in the "Writings" division of the Bible.

Noah, the hero of the biblical story of the flood.

Obadiah, prophet and author of the shortest book of the Bible (one chapter). He foretold the doom of the Edomites, the enemies of Israel.

Pharaoh was the official title of the kings of Egypt.

Philo, known as Philo Judaeus, lived in Alexandria, Egypt, and died in the year 50 C. E. He was a Jewish scholar and philosopher, a prominent leader of the Jews of Alexandria who, at that time, had a larger community than that of Jerusalem. Philo's religious theories were not in harmony with traditional Judaism, but leaned toward the Greek philosophy of the Stoics.

Rebecca, wife of Isaac. By showing kindness to the stranger Eliezer, she proved herself qualified to be Isaac's wife and to continue the tradition of hospitality as maintained in the household of Abraham.

Ruth, the Moabitish woman who was converted to Judaism. One of the sacred scrolls, "Ruth," gives a detailed account of her life.

Samuel, the last of the Judges. Before his birth he was designated by his mother Hannah to be a Nazarite (dedicated to God). He was a prophet and the founder of the prophetic guild. Yielding to a popular demand, he anointed Saul to be king of Israel; later on, when displeased with the ways of Saul, he predicted the fall of Saul's dynasty and secretly annointed David to be the future king. Two books of the Bible, Samuel I and Samuel II, are named after him.

Saul, the first king of Israel. He was an imposing figure, the tallest man in the land; he was an able organizer and a skillful warrior. Jealous of the successes of David and fearful of the future of his dynasty, Saul became moody and melancholy; he resented the friendship between David and his son Jonathan; he met with a tragic death in a battle with the Philistines.

Sokolov, Nahum, journalist and scholar, was born in Poland, in 1860. He was a Talmudist, an exponent of modern

Hebrew, and a great linguist. He settled in Warsaw and became the editor of the "Hatzefirah," a Hebrew daily newspaper. As an active Zionist, he was general secretary of the movement and editor of its publication, "Die Welt." He moved to London where he became the diplomatic representative of the Jewry of the world; he died in 1936.

Solomon, the wise king. Son of David, ruler of a united kingdom in Palestine. The best known monarch of the Bible. Builder of the first Temple at Jerusalem (about 1000 B. C. E.); author of books and epigrams.

Spinoza, Baruch, or Benedict, famous Jewish philosopher, was born at Amsterdam, November 24, 1632. He studied Talmud under Menasseh ben Israel. He became interested in philosophy and soon attained prominence as one of the most original thinkers of his age. He expressed heretical views, contrary to the traditions of Judaism; he also refused to believe in the Jewish theory of a personal God. He was summoned before the religious tribunal (Beth Din) of Amsterdam and, upon his refusal to retract his statements, was excommunicated on July 27, 1656. He left Amsterdam, took to lens grinding as a source of livelihood, and severed every contact with the Jewish people. Nor did he establish contact with the church. He was offered a professorship in philosophy in the Heidelberg University with the condition that he undergo baptism, but he refused the offer; he died at The Hague, February 21, 1677.

Vashti, the first queen of Ahashverosh, who was summoned to appear before the king but refused to do so. She was banished from the kingdom, and Esther was subsequently selected as her successor.

Zechariah, the second prophet of the "Return," lived in Jerusalem about 520 B. C. E. Like Haggai, he urged the people to proceed with the building of the second Temple; he visualized the day when the God of Israel will be the God of the universe; his book contains fourteen chapters and is included in the Book of Twelve.

Zephaniah, a prophet in Judah, was an aristocrat, possibly of royal blood; he denounced the vices of the royal palace; his prophecies are recorded, in three chapters, in the Book of Twelve.

296
P94